The Promise of Good Things

Floral Design for the Fall and Winter Holiday Season

Contributors

Authors

James DelPrince, PhD, Associate Extension Professor, Floral Design

Tricia Knight, PhD, Research Professor, Woody Ornamental Plant Materials

Christine Coker, PhD, Associate Extension/Research Professor, Citrus and Cucurbits

Christian Stephenson, PhD, Extension Agent, Herbaceous Plant Materials

Photographers

Kevin Hudson

Tricia Knight

Produced by the Office of Agricultural Communications, Mississippi State University Extension Service.

ISBN: 978-1-7354103-1-9

Authors' Welcome

The fall and holiday season in the South is a beautiful time of the year. Many of us think of it in the context of those glorious months of gradually more tolerable temperatures, plus the fun events peppered throughout. We feel the fall season begins when the younger set goes back to school. Of course, this has nothing to do with cooler weather, sweaters, or leaf color. The first months of the school year can be sweltering. As for other signs of fall, many of us in the Deep South do not see fall leaf color until December.

The changes we do experience are social, centered around academics with a focus on young peoples' school activities. Back-to-school, football games, band and choir concerts, and the numerous activities that revolve around family life order the season's change and advancement toward the end of the year.

Given the warm and active start of the school year, what draws us into the season is the promise of good things, the anticipation and ensuing excitement that summer will give way to the sweetness of fall. We can dream about dinner on the porch without the dessert melting before we can finish it. The potential for gardening after 10 a.m. seems thrilling.

Southern gardens begin to relax from the pressures of heat and dryness, enjoying cooler temperatures and occasional, soothing rain. Flower and garden enthusiasts' minds imagine chrysanthemums, pumpkins, and floral designs in the colors of fall. Deep crimson, gold, and gingery-orange flowers fill flower shop windows. Nurseries and plant farms offer bronze mums and pansies and kale in jewel tones of royal purple, rose, and gold.

Fall is the time to find freshly stocked ornamental plants like magnolia and camellia, ready for the home landscape. Halloween and Thanksgiving are harvest-time holidays, and, accordingly, the season guides us in our choices of plant materials, colors, and patterns for floral design and gardening. As November advances, our thoughts turn to winter holiday plans. Get-togethers, menus, and decorating with ideas new—or tried and true—are at the forefront.

We hope this book provides you with floral design ideas and inspiration to grow the materials for those designs. The Mississippi State University Extension Service offers a wealth of information on these topics.

Contents

About MSU Extension 7

Fall: The Excitement Begins 10

    Welcome, Autumn 11

    Table Treatments 21

    Designs for Buffet Tables 27

    All About the House 32

Winter Holidays 42

    The Festive Table 43

    Party and Event Buffet Designs 59

    Winter Cut Flowers 64

    Fireplace Mantels 68

    Welcome, Christmas! 82

    The Living Room 92

    Bed, Bath, and Kitchen 100

    Poinsettia: Living Symbol of the Season 108

About MSU Extension

The Morrill Act of 1862 paved the way for establishing universities to educate students in "agriculture, horticulture, and the mechanical arts . . . without excluding other scientific and classical studies." The Agricultural and Mechanical College of the State of Mississippi near Starkville, now Mississippi State University, was established in 1878.

There quickly became a need for scientific research in agriculture to aid the growing nation. Mississippi Senator James Z. George introduced the first experiment station bill in 1885, and, after 2 years, the modified legislation became the Hatch Act, establishing the agricultural experiment station system. In Mississippi, this entity is known as the Mississippi Agricultural and Forestry Experiment Station (MAFES) and includes multiple centers and farms throughout the state.

With degree-granting universities in place and research-based information gaining a foothold, the need for delivering useful information increased. Initially, farmers' institutes, agricultural societies, and corn and tomato clubs filled information gaps at the local level. But the Smith-Lever Act of 1914 created a nationwide network called the Cooperative Extension Service. Extension is the bridge between experiment stations and the public, connecting people to knowledge based on research and best practices that improve lives.

Faculty and staff at the MSU Coastal Research and Extension Center conduct research and educational programs to encourage responsible stewardship of natural resources and improve the health and well-being of Mississippians. The MSU Extension Coastal Floral program is headquartered at this center located in Biloxi on the beautiful Gulf of Mexico coast. We offer floral programs for consumers, retail florists, and flower growers.

Gary B. Jackson, Director of Extension

Steve Martin, Associate Director of Extension

James E. Henderson, Head, Coastal Research and Extension Center

MSU Extension Master Floral Designer Program

Have you ever wanted to learn more about floral design but could not find the right resources? If so, the MSU Extension Master Floral Designer certificate program is the perfect fit. This program was developed to help people appreciate the beauty of flowers and gain confidence in creating and enjoying their own floral designs.

In this program of best practices and science-based information in floral design, participants gain the foundations necessary to create beautiful, long-lasting arrangements. We begin with clear, concise explanations about how to keep flowers fresh by understanding a flower's life process. Next, students learn about the materials and methods used to extend flower life. Many people can identify beauty in floral design, but our students learn what makes these designs beautiful. Delving into the design principles helps students learn to create beauty themselves, skillfully blending design elements to create stunning arrangements. Several hands-on projects allow students to practice working with fresh flowers, foliage, and the mechanics used to control stem placement.

For more information and to register for the Master Floral Designer program, see http://extension.msstate.edu/lawn-and-garden/floral-design.

MSU Extension Master Gardener Program

In exchange for 40 hours of educational training and a nominal fee, MSU Master Gardeners volunteer 40 hours of service in horticultural projects that benefit their communities. Our Master Gardeners are encouraged to stay active with the organization after training, returning 20 service hours and 12 education hours per year. This program helps Extension reach more people and teach them about the benefits of horticulture. Serving others provides a sense of pride in your work and your community, and a big plus is that Master Gardeners build a friendship community among themselves.

To learn how you can become a Master Gardener, see http://extension.msstate.edu/community/leadership/master-gardener or contact your county Extension office.

MSU Coastal Horticulture Research Units

Beaumont Horticultural Unit

One of the smallest yet most productive research farms owned by MSU is in Perry County in southeast Mississippi. Since 1970, its 20 acres have featured vegetable, fruit, and ornamental research studies for small-farm production. The farm includes raised beds, high tunnels, greenhouses, and row plots. Crops are monitored and evaluated to help growers and home gardeners identify the best varieties for the coastal region. Beaumont Unit Director Dr. Christine Coker leads an annual field day in early June that is open to the public and features a variety of speakers and demonstrators. Mike Ely manages the farm.

South Mississippi Branch Experiment Station

Initiated in 1918 as an agricultural research station, the South Mississippi Branch Experiment Station now features All-America Selections trials maintained in USDA Hardiness Zone 8b. Also located on the property are woody and perennial plant trials in cooperation with noteworthy arboretums and universities. Approximately 200 plant varieties are trialed annually. Blueberry research begun in the 1970s has resulted in proliferating commercial production in the Southeast. The trial gardens are open to the public daily during daylight hours. Dr. Tricia Knight is director of Coastal Horticulture Research. Scott Langlois, research associate III, manages this research station. Look for the station's field day annually in early October.

Fall: The Excitement Begins

Fall Porch Dreaming

The kids are in school; it's time to feather the nest!

Sling a big wreath on the door; oranges and golds show up best.

Mums in clay pots on the porch to overspill;

I think I'll add corn stalks! Do you think it's overkill?

Pumpkins—the fancy kind that are warty and flat—I want

a stunning display to stir neighborhood chitchat!

Welcome, Autumn

Woody Plants for Fall Decorations

Using woody plants for seasonal decorations, especially for fall and winter holidays, dates back to ancient times. It was believed that displaying evergreens during the colder months would please the gods of spring, giving them a comfortable abode for the winter.

Southern landscapes, both wild and cultivated, provide an abundant supply of design components for holiday decorating. While some people have access to plant material from native stands, the most reliable and renewable supply can come from skillfully integrating your favorite plants into your home landscape. By carefully harvesting decorative greenery from these plants, you can have a sustainable source of design material. Always remove greenery in a pattern that encourages the plant's healthy growth. Southern magnolias, hollies, and conifers provide some of the most common greenery for seasonal displays, but a number of other plants can add character to your designs.

Don't forget to use potted woody plants for fall decoration. Nurseries offer a wide selection of materials that can be displayed in pots, singly or in combinations. You can add them to your landscape as they mature. Since potted woody materials are often used in focal areas, be sure to replace them if they lose their aesthetic vigor.

Doorway Décor

Add color to your doorway in the fall season with plants and flowers. Natural decorations such as live plants, pumpkins, and dried canes with touches of permanent botanicals speak of the season's colorful exit from the hot days of summer.

What a relief it is to experience, or at least dream about, the cool fall temperatures. Gardening and yard work become more pleasant in October, so finding horticultural activities outside is natural for those who like to "dig in the dirt."

The garden can become ragged and leggy in the long, dry days of summer, so it's a good idea to clear away overgrown plants and prepare beds for fall and winter favorites such as pansies, mums, and kale. We like the idea of preparing the house itself for the cooler days of fall, starting with the front door because it is often the central focal point of the home landscape.

Decorating the front porch and doorway conveys hospitality and openness. When family and friends arrive at your home, seasonal floral designs welcome them in an unspoken way. Decorating with healthy plants and flowers increases the beauty in your neighborhood and shows your neighbors that you care, wishing them the good tidings of the season.

This front porch combines a variety of materials that will last for several weeks with little maintenance. Instead of traditional stalks of corn, we used cut sugar cane from a local farm. The farmer removed the sharp-edged foliage. We used cable ties to hold the canes together and surrounded them with magnolia, orange firespike, ligustrum, liriope, and chrysanthemum plants. Read more about magnolias in the *Winter Holidays* section of this book.

The wreath is Mississippi-grown muscadine with a bouquet of permanent botanicals attached. A selection of pumpkin varietals completes the display.

Chrysanthemum
(Chrysanthemum morifolium)

Chrysanthemums add bright color to the home and landscape just at the start of fall. While mums start growing in the summer, they flower in autumn. Chrysanthemums come in many different colors, from bright yellows and oranges to lighter pastels. Chrysanthemums may be solid or bi-color. Many of us purchase potted chrysanthemums in the fall and enjoy their color until they fade. Make sure your mums get enough water, as drought stress will lead to fading flowers.

Chrysanthemums also can be a wonderful additio to the landscape. Most mums purchased are not cold tolerant enough to survive winters in Mississippi, but they may come back and provide color in future years if planted in full sun with well drained soil. Cover plants with a layer of straw mu to give them a bit of added protection from the co Cut back chrysanthemums several times in spring and late summer to promote bushy and compact growth.

Firespike
(Odontonema cuspidatum)

Firespike is commonly known as an herbaceous perennial for most of Mississippi, being killed to the ground in hard freezes. However, it may persist as a shrub in protected areas or the southernmost parts of the state. It may reach 4 to 6 feet tall. The flowers are typically reds or purples, up to 3 inches long, and clustered in foot-long spikes. This plant is recognized as an excellent butterfly and hummingbird plant. It flowers best in full sun, but it will tolerate partial shade. It is very tolerant of pruning, and it makes an excellent cut flower. It can reseed in the landscape.

Japanese Ligustrum or Japanese Privet (*Ligustrum japonicum*)

A versatile landscape shrub in the South, ligustrum is tolerant of all landscape situations except chronically wet soils. This plant can grow 12 feet or more in the landscape and almost as wide. Leaves are opposite, 1½ to 4 inches long, ¾ to 2 inches wide, and a dark, glossy green. It can be established as a specimen plant, multi-trunked small tree, hedge or screen, foundation plant, or topiary. It is very tolerant of pruning.

'Nobilis' and 'Recurvifolium' are two very common cultivars for Mississippi. 'Recurvifolium' has a wavier leaf margin. There are some variegated selections, but they are much less common. The long stems and waxy leaves can be integrated into seasonal decorations.

Pumpkins

Pumpkins come in a wide variety of colors and sizes. There are several types of pumpkins.

GIANT PUMPKINS

Eye-catching giant pumpkins are often featured in fall displays, size competitions, and harvest festivals. Giant pumpkins come in a range of colors, from the familiar red-orange to pink-orange and white. These giants typically weigh between 30 and 100 pounds, but under favorable cultural conditions can grow significantly heavier. The current world record for giant pumpkins is over 2,000 pounds, a figure that has been increasing nearly every year. 'Polar Bear' (30 to 65 pounds), 'Big Moose' (50 to 125 pounds), and 'Dill's Atlantic Giant' (50 to 100 pounds, though 100 to 200 pounds is not uncommon) are examples of giant pumpkins.

JACK-O'-LANTERNS

A jack-o'-lantern is a carved pumpkin, turnip, or other root vegetable lantern associated with Halloween. Its name comes from the phenomenon of a strange light flickering over a peat bog, called *will-o'-the-wisp* or *jack-o'-lantern*. In horticultural terms, a jack-o'-lantern is a type of pumpkin. Generally smaller than giant pumpkin varieties, jack-o'-lanterns can range from 10 to 40 pounds. Some examples include 'Tom Fox' (10 to 16 pounds), 'Howden' (18 to 26 pounds), and 'Early Giant' (25 to 40 pounds).

PIE PUMPKINS

These pumpkins are smaller and are suitable for your favorite pumpkin pie recipe. They are bred and selected for flavor, dry matter content, sugar content, texture, and yield. Pie pumpkins range in size from 3 to 9 pounds. Examples include 'New England Pie' (4 to 6 pounds), 'Cinnamon Girl PMR' (3 to 6 pounds), and 'Winter Luxury' (6 to 9 pounds).

SPECIALTY PUMPKINS

This category is all-inclusive! From miniatures to giants and everything in between, there are so many varieties to choose from.

Miniatures

'Wee-B-Little' is a tiny, round pumpkin. Remarkably miniature, about the size of a baseball, it averages 3 to 3½ inches in diameter and weighs in at a mere 10 to 14 ounces. 'Wee-B-Little' has a slightly flat-round shape like a normal pumpkin, and its bright orange rind is smooth enough for painting.

'Baby Bear' is unique for its size and shape. The deep orange, 1½- to 2½-pound fruits are about half the size of a normal pie pumpkin. With slender, sturdy, easy-to-grip handles, they are very appealing to children. In addition to its decorative use, the flesh is good for pies, and the seeds are good for a roasted snack.

'Casperita' is a ½- to 1-pound, white pumpkin that has a strong, green handle and holds its color well. It makes a bright addition to a seasonal display.

Specialty Colors and Textures

'Galeux d'Eysines' averages about 15 pounds. Its special attribute is a blistered skin pattern resembling peanut shells. It is a unique heirloom variety with a flattened-globe shape and salmon-pink skin. While the amount of skin blistering increases with time spent on the vine, it is recommended to harvest at maturity because fruits can crack when overmatured. 'Galeux d'Eysines' is an ornamental with a lot of character but also lends good flavor to soups and stews.

'Musque de Provence' is also known as 'Fairytale', and the ribbed, flat, tan fruits average 8 to 15 pounds. Thick, deep orange, moderately sweet flesh is its trademark. In France, cut wedges are sold in supermarkets and farmers markets for cooking. In addition, this highly decorative variety can lend character to your late-season décor.

The bumpy appearance of 'Marina di Chioggia' makes an interesting yet subdued ornamental statement for fall. Its medium to pale green color is complementary to many display combinations.

Specialty Shapes

'Turk's Turban' is a colorful, buttercup-shaped fall display addition. With a prominent blossom end button, it is striped silver, green, and white with a scarlet top that measures 7 to 9 inches across. 'Turk's Turban' averages 3 to 5 pounds per fruit.

'Green Striped Cushaw' ranges from 7 to 25 pounds. It is a striking green-and-white-striped edible ornamental. Similarly shaped, 'White Cushaw' also has a crook-necked shape but only weighs 5 to 15 pounds. Both are suitable for ornamental display as well as cooking. Better suited for decorating, 'Autumn Colors Cushaw' boasts unusual, tri-colored fruits with green bottoms, light orange tops, and white stripes from top to bottom.

'Naples Long' lives up to its name! These large, peanut-shaped, Italian heirloom squash can weigh 20 to 50 pounds. The skin is a deep green that turns tan in storage. The flesh is bright orange, and the flavor is rich and very sweet. Fruits are so large that each plant averages only one fruit per plant.

Most garden pumpkins are planted for Halloween. Pumpkins planted in spring mature in midsummer, long before Halloween. If left in the garden, they rot, so they must be harvested and used or stored in a cool, dry place.

Pumpkins for Halloween are best planted in late June and early July. They require 90 to 110 days from planting to harvest. Most pumpkin varieties produce strong, running vines that require plenty of garden space. Some varieties are described as having short vines and are adapted to limited space. Pumpkins cross-pollinate with summer squash, acorn squash, vegetable spaghetti, and small ornamental gourds if they are growing nearby. This is of no concern unless you plan to save seeds for another year.

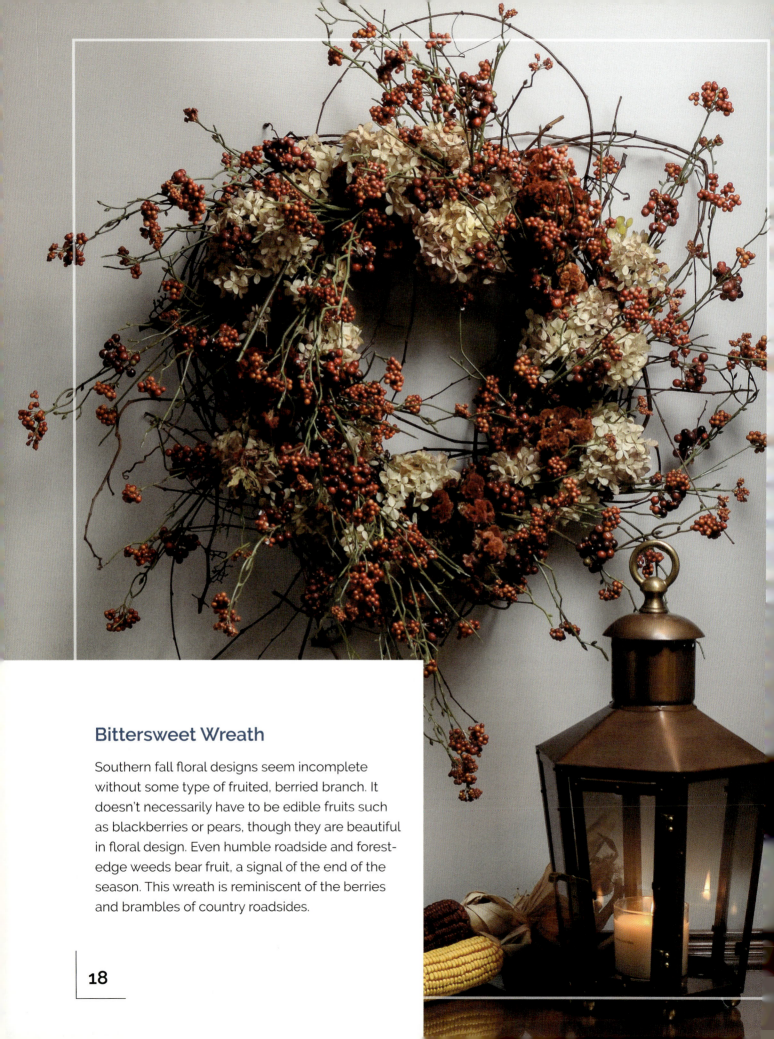

Bittersweet Wreath

Southern fall floral designs seem incomplete without some type of fruited, berried branch. It doesn't necessarily have to be edible fruits such as blackberries or pears, though they are beautiful in floral design. Even humble roadside and forest-edge weeds bear fruit, a signal of the end of the season. This wreath is reminiscent of the berries and brambles of country roadsides.

Our design began with a base of muscadine vine, harvested the previous winter and formed into a wreath right on the farm. We let some vines swirl beyond the confines of the circle, which gives the arrangement an informal look. We added dozens of artificial bittersweet stems to the ring as well as dried *Hydrangea paniculata* flower heads. The directional flow of the bittersweet is continuous, providing tangled rhythm and movement to the design.

For a refreshing addition to an interior room, remove an existing piece of artwork, whether photo, print, or painting, and replace it with a wreath for the fall season.

Panicle Hydrangea
(*Hydrangea paniculata*)

This species can grow quite large, reaching 20 feet tall and wide, but it is typically smaller in the landscape. It is another very traditional Southern landscape plant. Older bark may peel or exfoliate. Leaves are opposite to whorled, 3 to 6 inches long and 1½ to 3 inches wide. The flowers are white, and they mature to pinkish or purple. They appear in late spring and persist into late fall or early winter.

Flowers can be used fresh or as they dry into the fall. Some find the drying flowers unsightly, while others find them attractive in the fall landscape. This plant flowers best in the sun but will tolerate partial shade. Flowers are produced on the new growth, so prune in winter or early spring to avoid flower loss. 'Grandiflora' is an old selection, and the flowers can reach 12 to 18 inches long on well-maintained plants. Flower heads are heavy enough to pull the limb down in an arching manner. Many new cultivars are available, with some featuring darker shades of pink. 'Limelight', 'Phantom', 'Moonlight', and 'White Wedding' are newer introductions that are available for planting into the landscape.

Fall Decorating Supply Checklist

- ✓ Grapevine wreath
- ✓ Pumpkins, gourds
- ✓ Nursery plants (chrysanthemums, marigolds, foliage plants)
- ✓ Corn stalks, sugar canes, cotton stems
- ✓ Pots, soil
- ✓ Ribbon, raffia, silk flowers, wreath hanger

Ornamental Corn

Readily available at farmers markets and roadside stands at the end of summer, ornamental corn is a staple for autumn displays. Ears of ornamental corn vary in size, color, and even luster. Ears vary in size from miniature to more than a foot long. Kernels may be a single color or a mix of multi-hued nuggets.

'Glass Gem' produces 5- to 7-inch ears on 10-foot stalks. The kernels are translucent and rainbow-colored.

'Earth Tones Dent' has muted kernels, as the name suggests. Eight- to 10-inch ears grow on 8- to 10-foot stalks.

'Miniature Colored Popcorn' is a favorite for its mixture of bright, solid and multi-colored ears ranging in length from 3 to 4 inches.

Table Treatments

The Classical Centerpiece

Special events and occasions are made more special by the appearance of flowers on the table. The classic hemisphere design is a favorite for dinner parties and social events because it has a pleasing form and guests can converse over the flowers. Indeed, florists use this form regularly for table decorations, elevating the flowers on stands and varying the types of plant materials used. An experienced designer knows that you can always count on a classic to please.

Our design's silhouette is somewhat irregular, with some materials inserted deeper into the design while others extend outward lightly.

We selected orange lilies and dahlias because their advancing colors visually jump out from the design. Weighty, bronze chrysanthemums are tucked a bit deeper into the arrangement. Accents of pink-peach spray chrysanthemums, velvety dried celosia, and colorful nandina foliage add pattern detail.

The arrangement in this image would be beautiful for a club or hotel event, such as a birthday or anniversary party. Leave as-is for a brunch or luncheon or add brass candlesticks with fall-colored taper candles spaced around the design for nighttime shimmer.

Celosia
(Celosia cristata)

Celosias offer distinctive and beautiful flowers for the garden in outstanding colors, including bright red, yellow, orange, rose, magenta, and pink. The plant can grow to more than 3 feet, but dwarf varieties that reach just 4 to 6 inches are also available.

There are three groups of celosia, separated according to their flower shape. Plumed celosias have feathery heads made up of many tiny flowers. The cristata group is often referred to as cockscomb because these flowers resemble a rooster's comb; the complex flower shape makes an interesting addition to any display. Spiked cockscomb, or wheat celosia, has a narrow, spiky flower head with many flowers. These may have a shrub-like appearance because of their many flowers and attractive foliage.

Celosia is easy to grow from seed and will thrive in difficult soils as long as it is planted in full sun.

Dahlias
(group)

Dahlias provide fantastic flowers in the garden if they have good soil and water conditions. In return for the effort of growing them, gardeners are rewarded with spectacular blooms that can be as large as 15 inches. High temperatures can be a challenge for dahlias in southern Mississippi.

Dahlias are planted as tubers, and plantings in April and May will have peak blooms in September and October. If planted earlier, you can take cuttings in early summer to allow for a late-flowering crop.

For best results with dahlias, plant in full sun and make sure the soil is loose and well-aerated with plenty of organic matter. Ideally, dig down to 18 inches and add additional organic matter such as peat moss or compost. You may need to stake plants with large blooms to keep them upright.

Fright Night

Floral design themes need not be geared only for adults and special occasions. Whimsical themes have an appeal for mixed groups of adults and children. Halloween themes are fun, from cute and lighthearted to dark and scary.

In this design, a collection of on-hand Halloween objects come together with fresh flower stems and dried twigs from the yard. According to the floral design technique *unity by proximity*, individual materials contribute to a harmonious appearance merely by being placed closely together.

Floral design centerpieces need not be expensive. Gather up Halloween decorations from storage and take a fresh eye to objects in your home that are black or orange. They can contribute to a tablescape certain to send shivers down your spine!

These arrangements were created in scale to the Halloween gnomes, all set for their trick-or-treating. We used Mississippi-made floral containers made from twigs and moss for an earthy base. Fresh flower foam holds the flowers in place. Among other flowers, these designs contain lava-hot safflower, jaundice-yellow craspedia, and poison-green chrysanthemums.

Fresh Flower Food

The three chief components of fresh flower food are

1. Carbohydrates—sugars that provide flowers the energy to bloom
2. Citric acid—an acidifier that aids water movement into the stem and keeps vase water cleaner longer
3. Biocide—an agent that slows microbial growth that can clog stem vessels

Fresh flower food does work, but be sure to follow the manufacturer's mixing directions for best results.

The Old Farmstead

It can be hard to find time in our busy, modern lives for designing with flowers. Instead, try making attractive seasonal arrangements using permanent materials. It is rewarding to make a design with materials you love in the colors of the season.

Feel free to design and display permanent fall botanical arrangements early in the season—after all, when you design flowers for yourself, there is only one person to please. Use "back to school" days as the signal to decorate for autumn!

Permanent flowers and fruit are lightweight, so it is important to use a heavy container such as this terra cotta bonsai one. We arranged yellow-green apples and rusty pears so that their stems pointed in different directions, creating a series of haphazard, casual lines. A fretwork of muscadine vines arch over the fruit and provide a framework to hold permanent botanical bittersweet climbers in place. Dried yarrow flowers create a warm bed of color around the fruit. If desired, add a few pieces of cider-scented potpourri for fragrance.

Ammobium Table Runner

Try making a table runner from dried flowers this year—no intricate mechanics needed. Merely cluster dried flowers in bunches and place them one atop the other, from each end of the table toward the center. We paired the flowers with brown and white transferware.

Ammobium alatum is a prolific flowering plant and dries quite easily. It will produce the greatest number of flowers if grown in full sun. After harvest, place about five to ten fresh stems together, bind with a rubber band, and hang upside-down in a warm, dry space out of sunlight. The naturally papery flowers will dry thoroughly and be ready to use in designs in a few weeks.

Chrysanthemum Time

Pine cones scattered on beds of dry straw,

twigs, mosses, evergreen needles.

Birds quickly fly, dart around the changing garden.

A light, cold breeze,

fall fragrances,

the sounds of dried weeds and grasses singing in the musical wind—

it's chrysanthemum time.

Design Display Technique

Component designs—the use of multiple units grouped to make a single design

When the need arises to decorate varying-sized tables, create multiple small floral designs. Larger tables can hold several arrangements scattered along the center, while bistro tables look fine with just one.

See next page.

Dried Flowers on Mini Pumpkins

We learned how to make these sweet mini pumpkin designs from Mississippi flower farmer Tanis Clifton from Tishomingo County. Glue Spanish moss in place using cold floral glue or a similar adhesive. Next, glue dried flowers into the moss. We paired Mississippi-grown everlastings with commercially grown bunny tails from Italy. If displayed out of direct sunlight indoors, these little beauties will last for months. These arrangements are perfect for showers, fall weddings, or individual gifts.

Designs for Buffet Tables

Social Arrangements:
The Art in Entertaining

Southern-style entertaining requires flower displays—it's a must! An important component is using local foliage in the design to give it "Southern flavor." This is a technique used by generations of professional floral designers to make their designs look like their clients casually gathered flowers and arranged them themselves.

Creating a massive floral arrangement is not as difficult as it may seem, but it is important to master stable floral mechanic construction. Secure, reliable mechanics keep floral placements intact and provide ample water supply to cut flowers.

This arrangement includes a variety of jewel tones that would be so lovely for a party or reception. The bright, golden-yellow foliage is the holly *Ilex cornuta* 'O'Spring'. Learn more about this and other hollies in the *Winter Holidays* section of this book.

Glossy Abelia
(Abelia x grandiflora)

Glossy abelia is a versatile shrub common in many older Southern landscapes. It can reach up to 6 feet tall and just as wide. This plant tends to be multi-stemmed with branches that have an arched appearance and long shoots that can be incorporated into holiday decorations. Depending on your location, glossy abelia may be completely deciduous, semi-evergreen, or completely evergreen. Leaves are small, ½ to 1½ inches long, and a lustrous dark green throughout the spring and summer, transitioning to shades of bronze in the fall and winter.

Flower sepals may persist into the following spring in shades of rose and purple. Flowers are whitish to pale pink, tubular, and ¾ inch long. Although glossy abelia comes into flower in the late spring, flowers can last through frost in Mississippi. Development of new introductions such as Confetti™ or Mardi Gras™ with variegated foliage or 'Canyon Creek' with yellow leaves has renewed interest in this traditional plant. It can be used in small groupings or mass plantings in the landscape.

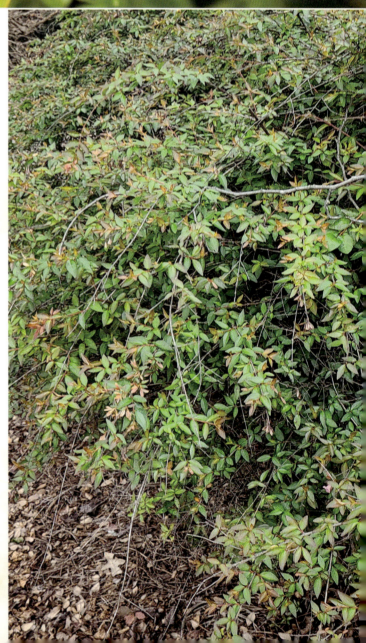

Fresh Flowers on a Pumpkin

A perfectly placed pumpkin proudly wears a crown of bright, autumn hues in this simple-to-make arrangement. All you need is a bunch or two of market flowers, a few snippets from the garden, and a small block of fresh flower foam.

It is not necessary to glue the foam to the pumpkin—just contour the foam to fit the pumpkin's indentation.

If the pumpkin has a stem, you can stick the foam on it for stability.

This arrangement lacks a water reservoir, so we compensated by selecting long-lasting flowers. Yellow marigolds and pinkish-orange carnations combine with ruddy, dried strawflowers and a misting of pink muhly grass. This design can be made up the day before an event if kept cool and out of strong sunlight.

Marigolds
(*Tagetes* spp.)

There are several species of marigolds we often use in our gardens. All marigolds are members of the genus *Tagetes* in the family Asteraceae. Often called the African marigold, *Tagetes erecta* is native to Central America. This marigold produces large, often double-globed blooms in yellow, orange, or white. These large blooms give the plant one of its other common names, the big marigold. Plants grow from 1 to 4 feet tall.

The French marigold, *Tagetes patula*, is a compact plant that is much shorter at 6 to 12 inches. Flowers of the French marigold may be yellow, orange, red, or bicolor. Marigolds will thrive through summer all the way to first frost if planted in full sun and watered well. Deadhead spent blooms to keep them producing their beautiful flowers.

Stacked in Our Favor

We used the same concept from the previous design but took it up a few notches. We layered fresh flower foam between the pumpkins as a water source for flowers and greenery. Many pumpkin varieties have flat or concave tops, making them stable when stacked. You can insert four to six bamboo skewers between each layer to anchor the pumpkins in place.

This arrangement is perfect for the buffet table because it brings color and pattern upward, away from the serving pieces on the table's surface. This design can be made with dried flowers instead of fresh for a long-lasting presentation. You can create the design at home, disassemble and pack the components, and then quickly reassemble it at the event space.

Impromptu

Having some friends over for a football watch party? Be sure to add some flowers to the mix to make your table the MVP.

For a fast fix, consider going bold and minimalistic. Large, glass jugs with narrow necks are perfect for single branches or a few cut flower stems.

This example illustrates a lot of show for the money, considering the prolific growth of nandina in the Southern landscape. Not as

long-lasting as some garden greens, nandina more than makes up for this fault with other attributes. The beautiful color display and luxuriant growth allow it to be used on its own, and it always gets rave reviews from flower enthusiasts.

We like lilies in the fall because their color range, availability, and lasting quality are just what is needed in floral design. You can purchase them in tight bud, with just a hint of color showing, and enjoy your arrangement for up to 2 weeks.

Nandina, Heavenly Bamboo
(*Nandina domestica*)

Nandina is a classic Southern landscape plant often seen around older homes. When not maintained, taller cultivars can have a weedy appearance with their bi- and tri-pinnately compound leaves clustered above multiple bare stems. The species may reach 6 to 8 feet tall. Leaves may reach 12 to 24 inches long and wide. Most new plantings are smaller selections, and this plant can be used in many landscape situations. It is very tough and has few problems in the landscape. The foliage is very fine-textured, and the leaves of many selections redden in the winter. Fruit appears in the fall and stays throughout the winter. It is generally red to reddish-orange, although there are selections with off-white or yellowish fruit. The plant does sucker and can also spread from seeds, but not all selections produce seed. Both foliage and fruit can be used for decorations.

All About the House

Autumn Joy

Fresh floral arrangements have a place in the home as decorative accents. They are refreshing and eye-catching. An end table is a perfect place for such a design, underneath an illuminated lamp. The lamp is the dominant item in the composition in terms of its size and glow, but the floral design delivers the elements of color and fragrance. The pool of light cast from the lamp illuminates warm-colored flowers like these rose-toned chrysanthemums, oxblood celosia, and maroon hypericum. To give the design a contemporary twist, we spun a defoliated kudzu vine around the flowers for visual motion.

Lidded containers give designers the opportunity to create impactful designs with many or just a few flowers. Some containers, like this darling white pumpkin, have a wire prong that holds the lid securely in floral foam. A trio of these designs would be terrific as a table centerpiece, each one a slightly different variation on the theme.

Orange Lily Ikebana

Ikebana, the Japanese art of floral design, is hundreds of years old. There are many schools of ikebana, each with its own rules and guidelines. Many ikebana teachers encourage simplicity in design, with reverence for all aspects of nature, including imperfection.

One of the greatest challenges in floral design is restraint, and some floral containers call for it. This little vase, a treasure by Mississippi ceramicist Jason Wilson of Sumrall, has a range of perforation sizes in its top, allowing for a wide variety of floral placements. We felt it was worthy of a special platform and chose this Asian ebonized rosewood flower stand.

Floral accents like this bring freshness to the library, office, or bedroom. A simple and lovely way to welcome holiday guests to your home is to place a small arrangement on their bedside table. Touches such as this take little time yet mean so much to friends and family.

Lily Anthers

The brown appendages in this photo are anthers, one of the reproductive parts of a cut flower. As they develop, they bear pollen that, in turn, aids in fertilization of the flower. Flowers have evolved to do just that—facilitate fertilization and develop seeds.

Floral designers should try their best to slow this process because it causes microscopic wounding of the stigma, the long stalk in the center, hastening the flower's death. When the plant no longer needs its showy petals and sepals, it begins putting its energy into producing seeds. An easy way to slow this process is to remove the anthers. Simply pluck them with your fingers as soon as the flower begins to open, before the anther "ripens" and bears its clingy pollen.

Pollen is also problematic when it comes in contact with flower petals, textiles, and other surfaces. If this occurs, do not brush off the pollen with your fingertips. Skin oils help to set the pollen stain, making it more difficult to remove.

Instead, brush the pollen off the surface using a chenille stem (craft pipe cleaner) or similar brush. Some designers have had success with placing stained fabrics in strong sunlight so that the pollen grains dry and become easier to brush away. Remember, it is always best to remove anthers once lily flowers begin to open.

Apple for the Teacher

Fall symbols are features in floral arrangements of the season. Apples bring to mind the cool days of autumn, and so do gourds. This tan-colored, apple-shaped gourd (*Lagenaria siceraria* 'Appalachin') is grown at Doyle's Coastal Ridge Farm in Picayune. In its fresh state, it is striated with mid- and light-green

markings but, when dry, takes on the color of leather. Some paint these in various red colors or even gold. We kept ours in the color that nature provided, using it as the focal point for our fall arrangement.

Asymmetry in flower arranging recalls Midcentury Modern design styles. With the advent of fresh flower foam, floral designers began to experiment with visual weight distribution in floral design, melding Eastern ikebana with European mass floral design. The result was line-mass and its distinct, triangular shapes. The placements of pineapple guava foliage create asymmetry in this design; without them, the arrangement is symmetrical. A blue-green McCarty pottery bowl from Merigold, Mississippi, complements the amber and tawny golds of daisies and standard chrysanthemums.

Pineapple Guava
(*Acca sellowiana,* formerly *Feijoa sellowiana*)

This is a large plant that is best suited for screens and hedges. It can reach 15 feet tall over time, with a spread of 10 feet. It is susceptible to cold damage, and that can limit its size. The leaves are opposite and evergreen. The top of the leaf may appear almost bluish-green, while the lower surface is silvery-white. This color combination makes it a versatile plant for decorating. The flowers appear in late spring and have numerous reddish stamens, giving them a fine-textured, tropical look. The plant will develop fruit from time to time with cross-pollination, and it reportedly has a pineapple flavor when ripe. It is grown commercially as a fruit in some countries.

Bundled Bounty

When designing with dried floral materials, it is possible to achieve interesting effects by arranging entire bundles of them rather than individual stems. Of course, this requires more materials, which is better for flower farmers' sales but can be challenging for flower arrangers' pocketbooks. A possible solution is to gather materials from your garden as the flowers naturally dry.

This design shows pre-bundled daylily (*Hemerocallis fulva*) and northern sea oat (*Chasmanthium latifolium*) stems secured to fresh flower foam mechanics. Daylily scapes (flower stalks) dry in place and are easily harvested. They provide the same effect as cinnamon sticks or expensive dried twigs in designs.

Our friends Carl and Dixie Butler, long-time owners of the Temple Heights home in Columbus, Mississippi, used to combine these from their lush gardens with permanent botanical flowers and berries to create realistic fall arrangements. The historic home was open multiple days per week and often hosted events. The arrangements displayed in their home were natural in appearance, especially with period lighting, and highly practical because they lasted the entire season.

In our modern example, we placed several dried bundles on the diagonal to form the design. Note that the entire stem of the dried material is important in creating the design's form. After this step, we added fresh flowers (marigolds, chrysanthemums, billy buttons, and solidago) for bright fall color.

Daylily
(*Hemerocallis* spp.)

Daylilies are popular perennial flowers for the home landscape. There is a magnificent amount of diversity in this genus, allowing for differences in flower structure, height, color, and time of bloom. You can certainly find a daylily that suits your desires for the landscape. Varieties may grow as tall as 5 feet or as short as 8 inches, and blooms may be anywhere from 2 to 8 inches across. Though daylily flowers last only a single day, plants produce many buds, so the total bloom time of a clump may be 30 to 40 days.

Daylilies thrive in full sun and should be planted 18 to 24 inches apart. They will look their best in soil that is high in organic matter and with proper fertilization. Separate daylilies every few years to keep clumps from becoming disproportionate to other plants in the landscape. When their flowers become less showy, it may be time to separate clumps. This provides the opportunity to share these pass-along plants with friends and family.

Stick Style

You can make the most unique arrangements with just a few stems of grasses and other floral materials. In fact, these are the type of designs that are complementary to our busy lifestyles because the fresh materials dry in place and keep their appearance for months.

We gathered pink muhly grass, northern sea oats, yarrow, and balloon plant for this arrangement. Materials were arranged in the hand, taking care to keep like materials together within the design. We cut the stems with sharp pruners and placed them in a glass cylinder held within the rustic container.

This design would complement a home office, kitchen, or bath. Once the season is over, discard the dried flowers, knowing they will compost nicely and become an enriching soil amendment. This is part of the beauty of growing and arranging fresh flowers.

Artful Sunflowers

Vincent van Gogh painted two series of his iconic sunflower paintings, first in Paris and later in Arles, France, in the late 19th century. We are just guessing, but he could have arranged the flowers himself before depicting them in his art.

Sunflowers are challenging to arrange. Akin to working with a brilliant, headstrong artist, it is often best to let them do what they want to do. Allow the flower faces to turn as they may, with some facing to the side or even the back of the arrangement. They are heavy-headed flowers and, as such, require weighty containers. This earthenware French confit pot was originally used to cook and store food preserved in duck fat, then buried in the ground to the glazed line to keep the edible contents cool. It was a ubiquitous pantry item of the time, but today it is a collector's item.

Why not try a sunflower arrangement yourself? Cut the stems and place them into a container, working from the outside of the pattern toward the interior. This is the reverse of arranging flowers in floral foam, where we often establish height first, then add placements to establish the design's width. The large flowers will gently fall to the container's edge; by designing this way, you will be working *with* gravity, not against it.

Sunflower stems are hairy and trap dirt and stem-clogging microbes. Re-do the arrangement every few days, sanitizing the container and adding newly mixed flower food to keep the flowers fresher longer.

Look for U-pick flower farms in your area, then block out a day on the calendar for harvesting and arranging. This is such a great activity to do by yourself or with a floral-minded friend. Don't forget to bring your pruners and a wide-brimmed hat—and plan a French-themed lunch.

Our arrangement is decidedly more abundant than many of Vincent's examples, but how could we resist our locally grown sunflowers?

Sunflowers
(Helianthus anuus)

Sunflowers are fast-growing annuals that bring a big statement to the landscape or floral arrangement. Many varieties are available, offering a range of flower sizes and number of blooms produced. While the traditional image of the sunflower is bright yellow, there are also wonderful options for sunflowers with deep burgundy and orange flowers. Note that the best varieties for cut flower use do not produce pollen. Check with seed companies that offer cut flowers for these types.

Sunflowers perform well when direct-seeded in the garden and will grow well in a range of soils as long as the area is not overly wet. When planting sunflowers,

Autumn's Overnight Parade

Halloween makes its way to the fall parade with
its jack-o'-lanterns and chilling movies.

The calendar turns to November,
and holiday plans start getting serious!

Thanksgiving menus and travel proposals:
the topics of conversation.

Wedding china is taken from storage,
tucked far within the cabinet.

Memories of Thanksgivings past
and departed family.

Sweet potatoes, auburn-orange.

Delicious fragrances from the kitchen;
spices and roasting meats.

As soon as it is cooked,
the meal finishes all too soon.

Dishes all done! Who will help decorate the tree?

place them 6 inches apart. Once plants emerge, thin them to allow 12 inches between plants. To keep sunflowers showing off through the growing season, plant seed every 2 weeks. This succession of blooms will provide ample cut flowers for the season. Sunflowers also do a great job of bringing wildlife into the home landscape—just be sure you are growing varieties that produce seeds.

Warm Regards

If you are a floral design enthusiast, embrace the challenge of creating a matching pair of floral designs. This is an advanced exercise, and mastering it requires some practice. Designs in pairs are quite useful for table decorations and allow you to use matching containers.

For those who like designing flowers for worship, a similar grouping can be quite beautiful if adapted to

a church altar. Ecclesiastical floral design is a unique art form, and many houses of worship require mirror-image arrangements flanking the cross or other sacred objects.

These designs were made in matching vases referred to as Bristol glass. Manufactured in the late 19th century, these items are often decorated with hand-painted patterns or scenes. We combined commercially grown cut flowers with locally grown foliage, both of which repeat colors found in the vases.

Much of the greenery was arranged first to create a gridwork of interlaced stems within the vase. These, in turn, hold the flower stems upright. We recommend avoiding chicken wire and tape mechanics in antique, painted containers. These items can scratch or otherwise remove paint and gilding. Repairs are possible, but restoration artisans are few and their work is understandably costly.

Winter Holidays

It's Christmastime!

The weather is changing, the winds pick up!
Shorter days, school holidays,
hot cocoa from a Santa cup.

Let's play outside and take a ride
on a sled if there is snow.
Collect the greens, ready nativity scenes,
and watch Grandma mix cookie dough!

The Festive Table

Pittosporum Garland

Late fall and winter celebrations run the gamut from seated dinners to family brunches to cocktail buffets. The season welcomes Hanukkah, the Jewish festival of lights. Special birthdays, bridal and baby showers, and other events give us reason to decorate using fresh foliage and flowers.

We chose a Southern cut-foliage favorite, Japanese pittosporum (*Pittosporum tobira*), and formed it into a garland to bedeck an antique chandelier. Pittosporum creates a lovely garland and is often overlooked for this application. It can remain fresh-looking for a day or two.

When making your own garland, harvest greenery with sharp pruners and place in a few inches of fresh flower food solution for an hour. This will allow the foliage to fully hydrate, filling the plant tissues with the maximum amount of water they can hold. Create the garland and refrigerate it in a plastic bag with aeration holes until needed.

Pittosporum
(*Pittosporum tobira*)

Pittosporum is an evergreen that is often used similarly to holly in many Deep South landscapes. While it can reach 10 to 12 feet tall and one and a half to two times as wide, many landscape cultivars are smaller. Leaves are obovate and 1½ to 4 inches long. Their color can range from green to green and cream variegations.

While mainly functional in the landscape, pittosporum can be integrated into seasonal decorations, adding contrast to designs. Pittosporum is considered hardy for USDA hardiness zones 8b and higher; it cannot be considered a reliable plant for north Mississippi.

Epergne with Blue and Violet Flowers

An epergne was often used on the dining tables of elegant Victorian homes. They were born from the accepted aesthetic of the time, that ornament added depth and interest to the overall appearance of any object or surface. We owe the regard and use of table flowers to the Victorians. Beyond love of ornament, a chief reason that flowers regularly made their way to the table is because dining styles changed in the 19th century, moving from the French style to the Russian. Instead of placing platters of meats and vegetables on the table, the new style called for serving pieces to be removed to the sideboard. Of course, sideboards were already around in the mid-19th century, but they grew larger in size and more ornate.

This epergne was filled with an assortment of blue and violet flowers, all of which would have been found in London and New York street markets in the 1800s.

The trick to arranging in this container is to limit the number of stems. Use just enough to suggest a geometric outline of the design, but keep space between the flutes so that their trumpet form is visible.

Delphinium
(*Delphinium* spp.)

Delphinium is a fall-seeded annual flower offering spikes of blossoms in fantastic colors—they may be yellow, pink, white, or a particularly striking true blue. Varieties of delphinium range in size from 3 to 6 feet and have excellent fine foliage that makes a good

The Flowers

Delphinium belladonna

Eryngium

Hyacinth

Lisianthus

Ranunculus

Scabiosa

background to plantings. Delphinium can be easily started from seed and thrive in areas that receive full sun. Local nurseries and garden stores often have transplants. Plant delphinium from November through February; it tolerates cold weather very well. Space plants at 8 to 10 inches apart. They may reseed in the garden. Areas where delphinium has reseeded may need to be thinned to avoid overcrowding. Adding additional organic matter to the soil and fertilizing can promote the growth of these flowers.

Three Kings Poinsettia Centerpiece

Few holiday decorations carry the tradition and impact of a poinsettia plant. The intense colors of their long-lasting bracts lend cheer to the home in the month of December. Easily procured from garden centers, greenhouses, and florist shops beginning around Thanksgiving, you can keep them looking their best by providing bright, indirect light and keeping the soil evenly moist but not soggy. This design features Princettia Red® poinsettias.

Our use of these plants can become more creative if we think about the necessary effect of a floral design combined with the specific needs of a site. In the home, we mostly avoid table centerpieces that block the interactions of people on either side of the table. Poinsettias grown in 4-inch-diameter pots are often just the right size for table centerpieces, but you should conceal their pots with a waterproof, decorative cover.

Begin the project with a 30-inch-long wooden board painted black and add felt feet to the base. Next, glue clear plastic liners to the top of the board, starting at the center, then spacing the remaining ones 6 inches apart. Next, staple artificial greenery to the top of the board, lightly filling in the spaces between the liners. Use hot glue to attach varying patterns of greenery along with artificial poinsettia leaves and bracts, pine cones, and red berries. Finish the construction with touches of woodsy mosses to provide texture. Water the poinsettias thoroughly, then drop them into the greenery base. Check the plants every 3 days because the small pots dehydrate quickly in the dry, indoor air. If the plants fade, replace them with similar plants or consider others such as cyclamen, chrysanthemum, or solanum (Jersualem cherry).

Holiday Greenery Serpentine Design

Evergreen foliage is a gift of nature to brighten your holiday decorations. For this design, we cut two fresh floral foam wreaths in half and adorned them with Southern greenery: boxwood, magnolia, and pittosporum. This irregular serpentine is a classic Baroque line, as rhythmic as a melody from a violin. It makes a lovely table centerpiece adaptable to seated dinners or buffets. If kept out of direct heat and sunlight and occasionally watered, this design can last the duration of the holiday season.

Many of these forms have papier-mâché backings that can soak up water and potentially damage wooden surfaces. You can use a protective layer of plastic, such as a shelf liner, to form a shield between the two. Following is a list of coniferous evergreen plants that are wonderful for holiday decorations.

Conifers

Conifers are the most widely used plants for holiday and Christmas decorating, with many homes choosing the fresh scent and beauty of a live tree, wreaths, or garlands. While many conifer products are grown in much cooler climates and shipped south for the holidays, the Southeast has wonderful options that can be integrated into the landscape.

PINES (*Pinus* spp.)
Mississippi is home to at least seven different types of pine trees. While these may not be deliberately planted into the landscape, many homesites have established pine trees on the property. Small branches can be harvested and used for wreaths or garlands, and cones can be integrated into those designs or used as ornaments.

EASTERN RED CEDAR (*Juniperus virginiana*)
When Mississippians cut their own Christmas trees from local forests, Eastern red cedar is generally what they select. These trees are evergreen, although they tend to dry out quickly when cut. Eastern red cedars have a classic cedar odor. Growth habit is highly variable, with some trees reaching 90 feet. Foliage color can vary from grayish-green to blue-green to light or dark green. Some cultivars are available.

ATLANTIC WHITE CEDAR (*Chamaecyparis thyoides*)
Another Mississippi native, Atlantic white cedar is found in low, boggy sites, freshwater swamps, and stream banks. This tree typically grows 40 to 50 feet tall and 10 to 20 feet wide in the wild, but many landscape selections are available that are suitable for almost any landscape situation; however, it is not very drought tolerant. Foliage color ranges from bluish-green to green.

CAROLINA SAPPHIRE ARIZONA CYPRESS (*Hesperocyparis arizonica* 'Carolina Sapphire', previously known as *Cupressus arizonica* var. *glabra* 'Carolina Sapphire')

This evergreen is a pyramidal tree that may reach 40 to 60 feet in height with a spread of 15 to 20 feet. The foliage color is a distinctive silvery-blue, and the color is consistent year-round. It has been grown as a Christmas tree in some areas, both in the field and as containerized plants that can be displayed for the holidays and then planted into the landscape. It does have a distinctive cypress fragrance and makes a unique addition to holiday decorations. It was developed by Clemson University and released in 1968.

LEYLAND CYPRESS (*Cupressus* × *leylandii*)

This evergreen is a hybrid between Nootka cypress and Monterey cypress, both native to the western United States. Leyland cypress can reach 60 feet or more in the landscape and has a pyramidal or columnar shape. Because it has a growth rate that may exceed 3 feet per year when juvenile, these plants are often used as screens and hedges in the landscape. Leyland cypress has a very feathery texture featuring green to bluish-green foliage, making it an excellent choice for holiday decorations. Leyland cypress is tolerant of both acid and basic soils but does require adequate drainage and full sun. It is susceptible to dieback from several pathogens. This plant is commonly grown as a Christmas tree in the Southeast.

MOMI OR JAPANESE FIR (*Abies firma*)

This evergreen features the classic foliage typical of firs used for Christmas trees without the tight foliage canopy and with somewhat sharper leaves. Foliage is dark green above with a lighter green underside. Although firs are usually dismissed in Southern landscapes as not being heat tolerant, this one can be grown across the Deep South. It can reach 40 to 50 feet in its native habitat, but Southern plants tend to be smaller. This tree is not known for producing cones in the South. Foliage can be used to make wreaths and garlands.

Evergreen Shrubs

FLORIDA ANISE (*Illicium floridanum*)

Florida anise is a large evergreen shrub that is native from Florida across to Louisiana. It can reach 10 feet tall with a slightly smaller width. Leaves are elliptical to elliptical-lanceolate and can be from 2 to 6 inches long. Anise is very shade tolerant and prefers moist to almost wet environments, making it a very versatile option for landscapes. Leaves tend to be lighter green as sun exposure increases. Leaves and stems are very fragrant with a licorice-like scent when broken or cut.

SMALL ANISE, OCALA YELLOW STAR (*Illicium parviflorum*)

Small anise shares many characteristics with Florida anise, although the native range is smaller. The two are easy to confuse. It can grow taller, up to 15 to 20 feet, and its foliage is somewhat darker. Small anise does tend to be a tougher plant and is more sun tolerant and slightly more drought tolerant than Florida anise. A relatively new cultivar called 'Florida Sunshine' has consistent yellow foliage and offers an interesting color splash for the shade and seasonal decorations.

BOXWOOD (*Buxus* spp.)

Boxwood has traditionally been a very popular plant for the landscape or as a cut material. However, in 2011, boxwood blight, a fungal pathogen, was identified in the United States. The disease is being closely monitored, and precautions are being taken. The disease has the potential to spread to all states. All plants in the boxwood family can be susceptible, and symptoms include defoliation. The disease is highly contagious and can even be transferred in cut boxwoods used for floral design. Researchers are actively evaluating species and cultivars for levels of resistance, and new selections are being released with less susceptibility.

When adding boxwoods to your landscape, always use the latest information regarding resistant varieties. Because it is a very fluid and emerging issue, we do not recommend specific cultivars. If you want to use existing boxwood plantings as a source of seasonal greenery, make sure the plants are well-maintained. Many larger boxwoods can have an outer layer of lush foliage covering a hollow inner core of leafless branches. Boxwoods have notoriously slow growth, and bare stems that are exposed while harvesting greenery for decorations may be visible for a long time; in some cases, they never get green again.

JACKSON VINE, GREENBRIER (*Smilax smallii*)

This evergreen vine is known across the South as both a weed and a coveted component of Christmas decorations. Leaves are a glossy green and plants usually have tendrils. Fruit may be present and ripens from green to red to black. Unlike its cousins, this species tends to have briars only at the base of the stem. The vine originates from a large tuber and can twine onto trees and shrubs to tremendous lengths, up to 30 feet long. It is valued as a food source for birds and other wildlife. In some areas of the South, it is used to frame doorways; in others, it is traditionally brought into the home for the holidays. It can become very weedy, overgrowing desirable landscape plants, the farther south it grows. It is more manageable in colder areas. It can be grown in the landscape with frequent maintenance or harvested from areas where it has become established as a weed.

Fortune's Osmanthus (*Osmanthus × fortunei*)
A hybrid of two different Osmanthus (tea olive) species, *O. fragrans* and *O. heterophyllus*, this large evergreen shrub can reach 20 to 25 feet tall. Resembling a holly, the young leaves are dark green and 2 to 4 inches long with 10 to 12 spines per margin. Mature leaves tend to be entire. This plant is a great choice for sunny landscapes, although it will tolerate shade. Osmanthus flowers in the fall, and flowers are white and highly fragrant but not very showy.

After-Dinner Craft

After the Thanksgiving meal, consider bringing out citrus fruits, cloves, and picks. Often, people are happy to help make these fragrant ornaments, especially children. This provides an opportunity to converse, make plans for the upcoming holiday, and share special memories. Place extra, completed fruits in produce bags in the refrigerator. When fruit on display begins to age, replace it from your fresh supply.

Studded Lemon Table Centerpiece

The fall and winter holidays center around the table, where we enjoy lunches and dinners with family and friends. This classic diamond centerpiece is akin to a short garland or table runner. Our selection of materials brings fragrance to the room without being overbearing. With care, a design like this will last for weeks, even into the New Year.

For this arrangement, you will need a variety of evergreen foliage, citrus fruits, cloves, wooden picks/skewers, and red ribbon. Use a variety of mixed evergreens from a florist that include Douglas fir, variegated holly, and eucalyptus. We added small-leaved magnolia for a Southern touch. Before you make the design, stud the citrus fruit (lemons, small oranges, and limes work well) with cloves. Use a pick to make a small starter hole, then add the cloves, one by one.

Free-float a brick of fresh flower foam. Remove the corners of the form to create a rounded shape. Adhere it within a plastic container using florist's wire. Insert 15-inch-long red taper candles into the foam using plastic candle picks. We cut about 1 inch from one of the candles to establish asymmetry.

Make the first placements, establishing the length and width of the overall design. Keep the design very narrow to leave room for china and stemware on the table. Consider making the design one-third the length of your table. This will leave room for end-of-table place settings and serving dishes. Importantly, keep these first placements low so that they rest on the rim of the container and angle downward. Each placement should be impaled into the foam at least 1 inch. Create an apron of greenery around the container's rim to establish the diamond pattern.

One of the challenges of this arrangement is to keep foliage placements very low in the design's center, where the candles enter the foam. Do not allow foliage to touch the candles as this will cause a fire hazard.

After placing foliage in the center of the pattern, add some ribbon loops using wired wooden picks. They repeat the bright red color of the candles and take the place of fresh flowers in the arrangement. Add clove-studded citrus to the design. You may need to use two or three picks/skewers to stabilize the heavy fruit in the foam.

Fill in the rest of the pattern with evergreens, taking care to hide the non-decorative floral foam. Remember to add water to the container when your design work is completed. Check the water level a few times per week. Remember: Never leave burning candles unattended!

Pomanders

By definition, a pomander is a mixture of aromatic substances enclosed in a perforated bag or box and used to scent clothes and linens. Historically, they were carried as a guard against infection. More commonly, pomanders are clove-studded oranges used for the same purposes. The term may also refer to a box or hollow fruit-shaped ball for holding a pomander.

The term *pomander* comes from the Anglo-French *pomme de amber*, which literally means "apple of amber." (In Middle English, *pomme de amber* was modified to *pomander*.) Amber in this term may also refer to the early practice of including ambergris, a waxy substance from the bile duct of a sperm whale, in the fragrant balls.

Oranges have long been considered special holiday gifts. At the end of the 19th century in Europe, when the custom of gift-giving for Christmas had spread, the orange was a rare and expensive fruit. They were likely purchased from merchants who brought the citrus from places like Valencia, Spain, or Ivrea, Italy. Oranges became a luxury for families of modest means who reserved them as a gift for their children. Placing an orange in the toe of Christmas stockings may have had something to do with the legend of the three balls (or bags or bars or coins) of gold that the Bishop of Myra, the real Saint Nicholas, gave to three poor maidens to use as dowries.

Cloves (from the French word for nail) are actually dried flower buds from the *Syzygium aromaticum* plant—a kind of tropical evergreen tree found in African and Asian countries around the equator. They were a hot trade commodity around the 15th century. Of the family Myrtaceae, the small, reddish-brown flower buds are used as a spice. Cloves were important in the earliest spice trade and are believed to be indigenous to the Moluccas, or Spice Islands, of Indonesia.

Cloves alone are said to bring protection and financial luck to those who use them, and oranges have long been a good-luck gift around the New Year in many cultures. By combining these two natural good-luck charms into a fragrant pomander, you are sure to attract some positive energy!

Making an orange and clove pomander is easy:

1. Select a firm orange (or clementine, tangerine, or mandarin).
2. Use a toothpick to pre-punch holes or stick cloves directly into the rind. Another option is to remove the thin rind in a pattern of your choice, exposing the white pith to make inserting the cloves easier. (This is only recommended if you are not covering the entire fruit.)
3. Store in a cool, dry place to preserve the pomander.
4. For a stronger aroma, cover the entire orange with cloves, and then roll it in a mixture of spices, such as 1 teaspoon ground cinnamon, 1 teaspoon ground cloves, 1 tablespoon ground nutmeg, 1 tablespoon allspice, and ¼ cup powdered orris root. Leave the orange in the mix for a week, turning once a day.
5. Place your finished pomanders in a bowl, stash one in a drawer, or hang them for display and fragrance.

Once dry, a pomander can last for months (some even say years). To prevent molding and encourage pomanders to dry evenly and retain their scent for up to a year, shake each one in a plastic bag of powdered orrisroot or cinnamon before displaying. You may also store pomanders in a paper bag during the drying process.

Citrus Trees for Home Landscapes

Citrus trees add to landscapes not only through their great-tasting fruit, but also as beautiful, small trees that produce copious amounts of small flowers and a fantastic aroma. Citrus trees also provide excellent resources to bees and other pollinators and are important hosts for the caterpillars of the striking swallowtail butterflies that are such a pleasure to see in the garden.

Several types of citrus trees perform well in southern Mississippi landscapes and can be grown in containers farther north in the state. Satsumas are quite possibly the most popular of all citrus plants for home gardeners. These trees can be extraordinarily productive and have very sweet, tart fruit with an easy-to-remove peel. 'Owari' is a common variety, and 'Kimbrough' is a good choice due to its cold hardiness.

Grapefruit trees are also a very good option for home landscapes along the Gulf Coast. Like satsumas, grapefruit trees are cold hardy and produce excellent fruit. Both 'Duncan' and 'Ruby Red' are good varieties with moderately sized fruit.

Of the varieties of oranges, 'Washington Navel' is the best choice for growing along the Gulf Coast. This variety gets its name from a small, rudimentary fruit embedded at the blossom end of the orange. Plant oranges in a protected area, preferably on the southern end of the property.

Though not a true citrus, kumquats are also a great option. They are sufficiently tolerant of cold to rarely have problems along the Gulf Coast. The most common type of kumquat is 'Nagami', which produces an oval fruit, but gardeners may also be interested in 'Meiwa' kumquats; their fruit is smaller and round with an excellent sweet taste.

Lemons and limes are very sensitive to cool climates and must be protected from chills. Meyer lemons, which are a cross between a true lemon and a mandarin, are a good option because of their increased cold hardiness and sweeter, less acidic taste. Lime trees are the most sensitive to cold, so it is best to plant these in containers that can be moved to a protected area when temperatures drop. A hybrid of lime and kumquat, called a limequat, is more cold hardy and can be grown outdoors.

The best time to plant citrus trees is in January and February. Trees planted during this time will be better able to tolerate cold snaps before spring than trees planted before December. When choosing a citrus tree, look for one that is between 2 and 4 feet tall. Ideally, the tree should have three to four branches with a slight upward growth.

When planting citrus, be sure to give them plenty of room to grow, and keep in mind that different types of citrus will require different amounts of space. Kumquats, lemons, and limes need the least space and can be planted in a 15-foot circle. Satsumas will grow just a bit larger and should be planted in a 20-foot circle to give them plenty of room. Grapefruit and orange trees can get quite large and should be given a spacing of 30 feet.

Citrus trees will grow best in areas with good drainage and high organic matter. In areas with poor drainage or where there is heavy clay, citrus plants may perform better if planted in a mound or berm 8 to 12 inches high. Citrus trees thrive in full sun and, when possible, should be placed on the southern end of the landscape where it will generally be slightly warmer and the trees will have some protection from harsh northern winds.

Be aware of the cold hardiness for the citrus trees in your landscape, and take steps to protect them during cold weather. Kumquats are the most cold-hardy species and can tolerate temperatures as low as 16 to 17 degrees Fahrenheit. Satsumas can take temperatures as low as 18 degrees. Oranges and grapefruit may be damaged at 23 to 24 degrees, while lemons and limes may be damaged at 26 to 28 degrees. Severe cold damage may lead to the top of the plant dying back and growth of the rootstock. Plants will have large thorns, and you can trace the rootstock growth to the base of the tree below the graft scar. Fruit from rootstock growth will taste sour and have many seeds.

Oranges and grapefruit begin to flower in March, with satsumas and kumquats a bit later in March and April. Both lemons and limes will flower continuously, but they put on the most flowers in spring. Flowers are formed in small clusters on growth from the previous year or as single flowers on new growth. Often, gardeners are dismayed to see flowers dropping from citrus trees, but this is not a cause for great concern. Citrus trees will often drop flowers and fruit, and a good crop can be produced with only 1 or 2 percent of flowers maturing. Blossom shedding often occurs in the early spring, and fruit often shed in May or June when they are about the size of marbles.

You can pick satsumas and kumquats as soon as the fruit is at mature size. Taste is the best indicator that fruit is ready to harvest. Fruit left on the tree will turn from yellow to orange and develop a loose skin. Exposure to cooler temperatures will improve flavor. Pick all fruit before the coldest days at the end of January or in early February. Removing fruit by this time will improve the citrus tree's productivity the next season.

Throughout Mississippi, citrus, particularly small varieties like Meyer lemon, satsuma, and kumquat, can be grown easily in containers. This allows the trees to be moved indoors or into a small greenhouse to protect them from the cold. Citrus grafted to 'Flying Dragon' rootstock is significantly dwarfed and will perform very well in containers. Citrus trees are usually sold in 2- to 3-gallon nursery containers; move them to larger containers within the first year. The trees will generally need to be transplanted to larger containers every few years as they grow. In most cases, a 15-gallon container will accommodate the final size of the tree.

Silver Candlesticks

One of the quickest and easiest ways to bring holiday color to the table or other spaces in the home is through

adorned candlesticks. We often have items like these stored out of sight or even placed in display cabinets. Why not bring them to the forefront of holiday decoration?

We used narrow ribbon and tied fresh sprigs of holly and greenery on the diagonal line of our candlesticks, creating a dynamic secondary line to the overall composition. All it takes is a few snips from the yard and a shoestring bow! Gather a collection of mixed-and-matched candlesticks for an eclectic display.

Designer tip: This collection will look professional if you unify it through color. Add candles of any shape or size, but all in the same color. Consider white, red, pink—whatever works best for your home.

Chair Decoration

Make a special dinner guest feel even more so when seated in the chair of honor. You can easily construct chair decorations with materials you have on hand. We used three kinds of ribbon (sheer, glittered, and velvet) in three widths, repeating the lyre design of the chair's back. Paper-covered wire is the mechanic of choice; it will hold things in place without marring furniture finishes. Small bouquets of festive greenery add the Christmas touch. Think of this design idea for a dear grandparent, someone celebrating a birthday, or another honored person worthy of recognition.

Candles and Their Burn Times

Pillar	30+ hours
Votive, large	8–10 hours
Taper	6–10 hours
Votive, small	4–6 hours
Tea light	2–3 hours

Poinsettia Favor

Looking for an idea for a luncheon or dinner party favor? Consider a miniature poinsettia plant for guests to take home and enjoy. You can place several of these in the middle of the table as a centerpiece, then give them to guests when the party is over. We used a discount-store find—a pretty, gift-wrapped box—and lined it with aluminum foil. It makes a quick and perfect cache pot.

Winter Rose Centerpiece

Keeping flowers fresher longer is always a point of conversation for floral design enthusiasts. We have an idea that works well using the blossoms of 'Winter Rose' poinsettias. Studies have shown this specific flower to last over 2 weeks when cut and placed in water. We prepared our version as a low-profile table centerpiece that requires few materials.

Gather the ingredients for this design:

- Tin floral container with plastic liner
- Waterproof tape or household tape
- Fresh flower foam
- Floral pruners
- A variety of evergreens from the landscape. We used
    - Leyland cypress
    - 'Little Gem' magnolia
    - Boxwood

First, cut individual stems of 'Winter Rose' poinsettias from a potted plant. This is the easiest way to procure them because they are not commonly sold as cut flowers. Take care to cut the stem at the proper length for the arrangement. Poinsettias are members of the Euphorbia family and, as such, exude white latex. The more latex the flower "bleeds," the more it will wilt. Remove any leaves that may be pressed into the foam.

Place cut poinsettia stems in water to fully hydrate. If you have fresh flower food on hand, be sure to use it to aid water uptake. Let them drink water for at least 1 hour before arranging. Do not store these flowers in refrigeration; poinsettias like temperatures above 40 degrees.

Hydrate fresh flower foam using the free-float method. Once it is hydrated, cut it to size, place it in the liner, then tape it in position using waterproof tape. Next, place the foam-filled liner into the tin container.

Be sure to add water to the liner within the container before arranging. This is in addition to the water the foam already holds from the free-float hydration. Fresh flower food solution is recommended.

Create the pattern of the design, establishing length, width, and height. Be sure to impale cut stems at least 1 inch into the foam to ensure stability.

Follow the confines of the pattern size you have established in the previous step. Note that a variety of foliage patterns and textures make the design more interesting and attractive.

We added three 'Winter Rose' poinsettia blooms in a line down the center of the arrangement. Note the facings of these flowers: the center flower looks to the ceiling, while the remaining are faced to the left and right.

Keep this arrangement out of direct sunlight and drafts. Remember to add water to the container, checking it every other day or so.

The Floral Enthusiast's Wish List

- Floral containers (ceramics, baskets, antique epergne)
- Floral design mechanics (foam, tape, wire)
- Floral knife
- Flower press
- Garden gloves
- Jardinieres and cache pots
- Pruning shears
- Scissors
- Trowel

Party and Event Buffet Designs

White and Pink Buffet Design

Flowers and floral containers can evoke dear memories when chosen for holiday display. As the seasons progress, we think about our ancestors—parents, grandparents, and the generations who made our families who we are today. The floral decorations we create using their favorite flowers and treasures bring them back to us in much the same way as serving foods using time-honored recipes and cherished dishes.

This planter was a flea market find, displayed on a table near a dented aluminum watering can and a wooden pitchfork. It may have lived its life on the front porch of a Southern home for nearly 100 years. Imagine the plants it held over the years! Boston ferns, asparagus ferns, geraniums, or impatiens?

We gently washed its time-worn surface with a mild soap, then added felt feet to the base to avoid scratching the table. We placed a floral foam-filled plastic container inside it, then arranged the fresh flowers and greenery.

Feminine flowers contrast with the patinated container using a palette of creamy white *Hydrangea macrophylla*, LA hybrid lilies, and roses combined with soft pink peonies, Ranunculus, and king protea. Fluffy Limonium adds an antique gray tone to the floral arrangement. The broad strokes of magnolia declare the design "Southern."

Many of the flowers used in this arrangement have enjoyed newfound popularity in weddings and events. They were commercially produced by experts with many years of growing, harvesting, and shipping experience.

A Southern Wedding

Winter weddings provide the opportunity to showcase white and cream floral decorations accented by Southern greenery. Commercially grown flowers, shipped from California, South America, and Europe, offer a wide array of options.

We added locally grown foliage to our setting by incorporating Elaeagnus, ivy, and yellow holly berries. The balmy whites of cream stock, ivory roses, and glowing holly visually warm the design, a good technique to remember when using white designs at dreary winter events. Conversely, in the hot summer, icy whites with greenish undertones cool down a setting and provide guests with a visually refreshing composition.

Learning about Floral Design

Floral design is best learned in a structured environment where participants gain knowledge about floral care, handling, and design mechanics. Without mastery of these and other foundations, you will miss important pieces of learning.

- The MSU Extension Master Floral Designer program delivers measured content, allowing you to grasp and understand the material in just the right amounts.
- Mississippi State University is a national leader in floristry education, with the floral management concentration in the horticulture major leading to a Bachelor of Science degree.
- Floral wholesalers hold day-long design demonstrations with noteworthy speakers.
- Garden clubs offer a wealth of educational programs, demonstrations, and shows.
- Nearby colleges and continuing education programs offer helpful learning resources.

Wedding Flower List

Antirrhinum majus	Snapdrago
Consolida majus	Larkspur
Elaeagnus pungens	Elaeagnus
Hedera helix	Ivy
Ilex	Holly
Matthiola incana	Stock
Rosa sp.	Rose

When not displaying Yuletide pastries, vintage cake stands provide an ideal pedestal for holiday flowers. We continued the floral theme of our design pair, making use of small cubes of fresh floral foam to keep roses hydrated for up to 2 days. A design like this uses fewer flowers than you might think. The idea is to allow about 20 to 30 percent of the container to be seen. This keeps the arrangement from being too massive and allows the wispy lines of materials, such as the variegated ivy, to add drama and flair.

English ivy
(*Hedera helix*)

The potential uses for decorating with English ivy are endless, but be careful when planting in the landscape. In beds, the height is limited to less than a foot. However, it is a climbing vine and will readily use any available structure or plant as a trellis. It does attach itself to its supports, and it can damage structures. It can also smother other plants. It is evergreen and flourishes in sun or shade. You can also grow it as a houseplant. The leaf shapes vary greatly with different cultivars, from deeply to gently lobed, and leaves may reach 6 inches long. Leaves may be solid light or dark green, or variegated with patterns of cream or yellow. Leaves of older vines lose their lobing as they mature and can be valuable as filler in arrangements. Consider planting ivy in an upright container such as a tall pot or trough. The cascading stems are clean with leaves oriented in a pleasing, rhythmic manner.

'Autumn Leaves' Topiary

One of the reasons that red-and-green decorations are popular for Christmas is the strong contrast between the two—they are direct complements on the color wheel. Taking this notion further, use color contrasts in your floral design work, but change up the usual color traditions.

The poinsettia in this design, 'Autumn Leaves', is one of our favorites. Its intense color combination of shrimp

and gold (red-orange parent color) glows. We paired it with Douglas fir, using mostly the undersides of the branches to showcase its blue-green color.

Once the materials are assembled, this large-scale buffet design is easy to make. We placed crumpled chicken wire in the ceramic pot with three dowel rods forming a tripod structure within for added stability, working the sticks through the wire. Next, we placed fir branches—leftovers from a nearby Christmas tree lot—into the wire netting, starting at the bottom and progressing toward the top.

We hot-glued 4-inch-long water tubes into the network of stems and wire, filled them with water, and add poinsettia blossoms. Dried orange slices and cinnamon sticks add holiday spice to the design. Overall, this arrangement provides maximum impact for little cost.

Winter Cut Flowers

Winter Cut Flower Favorites

Alstroemeria

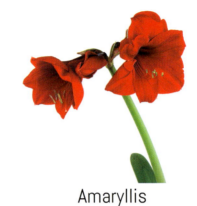
Amaryllis

Camellia

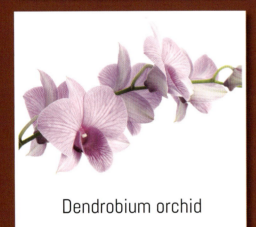
Dendrobium orchid

Gerbera

Hypericum

How to Care for Cut Flowers

You can use numerous types of cut flowers and berried stems in holiday decorations. Make a quick arrangement by placing a bunch of market flowers and some evergreens from the garden in a pitcher or vase. Use a container from your collection that you have never considered before.

Recut stems with a sharp knife rather than scissors. Scissors pinch water-conducting vessels and hinder uptake. It is fine to use pruning shears on woody plant materials.

Use the flower food that comes with your purchased flowers. It helps stems take up water and contains carbohydrate to help with bud opening and color retention and citric acid to help keep microbial growth in check. The third component, a biocide, helps keep vase water clean. Change the vase water every three days.

Cut flowers last longer in cooler temperatures. Even a few degrees can make a big difference.

| Carnation | Chrysanthemum, spray | Deciduous holly |
| Rose | Star of Bethlehem | Tulip |

One way to keep a cut flower or cut evergreen design fresh longer is to place it in an unheated garage or porch at night, as long as temperatures don't fall below freezing. Evergreens can tolerate temperatures a few degrees below freezing, but cut flowers are more tender and may freeze. Replace the design in its display area first thing in the morning when it can be enjoyed.

Forcing Bulbs

Some hardy bulbs can be "convinced" to flower by artificially exposing them to the right environmental conditions. This process, known as "forcing," provides fantastic color through the winter and into early spring. Tulips, daffodils, hyacinths, and crocuses are some of the most common bulbs for forcing.

When selecting bulbs, it is best to choose the largest ones because they will produce showier blooms. Bulbs for forcing can be potted from September through November, allowing 8 to 12 weeks of cold treatment for tulips, and 8 to 10 weeks for hyacinths, daffodils, and crocuses.

When potting bulbs, bulb pans are the best container choice. These clay or plastic containers are significantly wider than they are tall. As with any container, it is important to ensure good drainage. Some bulbs can be forced in water; choose a shallow container with a depth of at least 2 inches.

The ideal soil mix for forcing bulbs is light and well-aerated. An equal mix of potting soil, peat moss, and vermiculite or perlite works well. It is not necessary to use fertilizer in the soil because the bulb already contains all the energy it will need to produce a bloom.

Insert bulbs into the growing media so that approximately three-quarters of the bulb is below the soil surface. The neck of the bulb should be around 1 inch below the rim of the pot. Bulbs can be placed close together but should not be touching. Once the bulbs are set into the pot, add more soil mix so that only the very tip of the bulb is exposed. Water thoroughly and add more soil mix to account for settling.

The most important thing when forcing bulbs is to begin growing them in cool temperatures, allowing them to develop a good root system, and then move them to a warmer environment to stimulate flowering. It is important to provide the correct duration of cool temperatures. If they don't get a long enough cooling period, they often produce shorter stems than desired. On the other hand, bulbs that are cooled for too long may produce excessively long stems.

Temperatures for this cooling period should be between 35 and 50 degrees. Directions for forcing bulbs often recommend keeping bulbs outside to provide this temperature requirement. However, here in southern Mississippi, we rarely have these cool temperatures long enough to force bulbs. The easiest solution is to keep bulbs for forcing in a refrigerator. If you do so, keep them separate from fruits or vegetables that may give off a gas that can interfere with their development.

As the end of the cooling period approaches, check bulbs to make sure they have produced roots. Look for roots emerging from the drainage holes. Once you see emerging roots, you can move your bulbs to a brightly lit area with temperatures around 60 degrees. If the light in that area is from one direction, occasionally rotate the container to prevent the growing shoot from bending toward the light.

Keep an eye on the soil, and add water when it becomes dry. At first, the potted bulbs will not need much water, but you will likely need to water more frequently as the flower grows. Bulbs grown indoors may decline faster than those in the garden due to the low humidity and warm temperatures. Moving them out of direct sunlight and into a cool room at night will help prolong blooms.

Floriography: The Language of Flowers

We often give the gift of flowers to those we care about to show our affection and mark important occasions. The use of flowers to convey symbolic meaning has a long history. Flowers appear as important symbols in ancient China and Persia. In the Roman empire, roses were considered symbols of beauty and associated with the goddess Venus. Great victories were marked with the awarding of laurels. Olive branches have long been a symbol of peace. Flowers were especially important symbols in medieval Europe, often appearing as heraldic representations.

Using flowers to convey messages became extremely popular during the Victorian era in Europe, accompanying the expansion of commercial floristry. Flowers became symbolic of messages and emotions that were difficult, if not embarrassing, to put into words. The first of many floriographies, or dictionaries of flower meanings, was *Le Langage des Fleurs* by Charlotte de la Tour, published in 1819. Many upper-class families would have at least one floral dictionary, and interpreting the meaning of flowers was a hobby.

The acceptance of floriography created its own challenge because different books would offer different and often wildly contradictory meanings for the same flowers. As interest continued to expand, not only was the flower itself important in conveying meaning, but also its arrangement in a bouquet or where it was worn.

Likely the most familiar flower meanings known to us are the various colors of roses. White roses are associated with purity and innocence, while red roses are used almost universally to convey either love or congratulations. Yellow roses can convey friendship or admiration. Lavender roses are said to tell the recipient that you fell in love with them at first sight.

Chrysanthemums have also been sent as a message of love if the flower is red, but to denote truth if the flower is white. The two flower colors combined would convey true love for the recipient.

While we often associate flowers with romance, the language of flowers could also be used to send messages to friends and even to indicate disregard. Bells of Ireland, or yellow lilies, could show gratitude. Euphorbia could encourage a friend's persistence. Sage could be sent to compliment the recipient's wisdom. Depending on the floriography used, a gift of hydrangea flowers might signal acceptance of an apology, or it could imply vanity. Snapdragons can be used to indicate graciousness but might also imply deception. Begonias, rhododendron, and oleander may be included to send a cautioning message, and asphodel or rue for regret. More pleasantly, daffodils convey that the sender feels the sun shining on them when in the presence of the recipient.

While there are many meanings and different interpretations attributed to flowers, they remain one of the most meaningful gifts we can give to brighten the day of friends and loved ones. A bit of floriography can add fun to designing and giving flowers.

Fireplace Mantels

Mixed Evergreens from the Southern Landscape

A combination of mixed cut foliage by itself should be considered for many floral design applications, but especially during the holidays. If arranged in a water source, the greenery has the potential to last 3 or more weeks on display. Of course, the temperature of the room, proximity to heat sources, and post-design care all factor into its longevity. It is a natural, unaffected look and is always an appropriate decoration.

When creating evergreen designs, allow Mother Nature to direct how each branch is featured. Slow down a bit and take a brief look at stems before positioning them in a design, particularly the first five or six placements. We found it was possible to create asymmetry and curved line in this design, created with three separate containers, each holding fresh flower foam.

Mixed foliage designs are highly unified by their green color. To make the design interesting, combine foliage with varying patterns and textures. Pattern is the outline or silhouette of the leaves and branches. Texture is the surface quality of the greenery. Some greenery is scaly (Atlantic white cedar), while some is glossy and reflective.

Note how some stems gently break over the edge of the fireplace. This technique softens the static line of the mantel and increases the dominance of the foliage in the composition. The result is a grand yet understated floral design.

Holly

Hollies, of the genus *Ilex*, are a diverse group of plants with a fossil record that dates to before the beginnings of continental drift. Today, they are native to and cultivated in both hemispheres in tropical, subtropical, and temperate climates.

Hollies may be evergreen (hundreds of species) or deciduous (around 30 species), and both types have some native representatives in Mississippi. Hollies can range in size from rare groundcover types to small shrubs or trees. Their flowers tend not to be very showy, but they are attractive to bees. Holly plants are either male or female, with only the females producing the showy fruit associated with the plant. Fruit can be red, black, yellow, white, or purple, but red is the most common (more than 80 percent). Regardless of color, holly berries are a food source for birds and other animals.

Hollies played an important role in the historical customs of the Druids, Romans, and Greeks, as well as Native Americans. The role of holly in Christmas customs and other seasonal decorations goes back to the Druids. They believed that the sun never deserted the holly tree, making holly a sacred plant. Homes were decorated with holly to give the woodland spirits shelter from the harshness of winter. Because of the spines, holly was believed to repel evil spirits in early Europe. Roman newlyweds were given holly wreaths as a symbol of congratulations and well wishes. In ancient floral vocabularies, holly represented foresight, and it was often combined with mistletoe, which represented the ability to overcome difficulties.

Many present-day holiday customs related to decorating with holly are associated with the ancient festival of Saturnalia. Occurring December 17–23, this holiday celebrated the god Saturn. Holly boughs and gifts were sent to esteemed friends as symbols of warm wishes. Mangers were decorated with holly sprigs in some parts of Italy to commemorate the birth of Jesus. Holly was even hung in stables, and cattle supposedly thrived if they saw it on Christmas Day. In England, holly sprigs with leaves and berries were placed on beehives to wish them a merry Christmas.

Design Principles for the Master Floral Designer

balance

proportion

rhythm

scale

unity

dominance

harmony

Jungle Gardens Selections

Jungle Gardens on Avery Island in south Louisiana was established by E. A. McIlhenny Jr. Several holly selections were released from plants curated by Mr. McIlhenny. While not as common in the nursery trade, which limits availability, it is interesting to include selections that were made at Jungle Gardens because of its proximity to Mississippi.

Holly leaves are symbolic of the crown of thorns placed on Jesus's head at crucifixion, while the white flowers represent purity and the red berries the blood of Jesus. Today, homes and churches are decorated with holly as a continued symbol of goodwill, and we are fortunate to have a wonderful assortment of hollies to lend a unique touch to Mississippi's holiday season.

American holly
(Ilex opaca)

Probably the first holly most of us think of for traditional holly decorations, this plant is native in the U.S. from eastern Massachusetts to Pennsylvania, West Virginia and south to Florida, west to Texas and Missouri, and north to Indiana, Ohio, and Kentucky. It is a common tree in mixed hardwood forests, and fruit ranges from red to orange or yellow and is 5/16 to 3/8 inch in diameter. While many cultivars exist, many American holly boughs for decorations are traditionally harvested from native stands.

'Avery Island'

(Ilex cornuta 'Avery Island')

'Avery Island' is a female Chinese holly that originated from a hedge planted at Jungle Gardens, and it was selected by E. A. McIlhenny in the 1940s. This plant forms a large, upright shrub that tends to have a loose growth habit. The leaves are a glossy dark green and 2¾ to 3½ inches long. Leaves may have one to seven spines, but a single terminal spine is most common. The plant tends to fruit heavily, and fruit is yellow and large, averaging around ¼ inch in diameter.

'E.A. McIlhenny'

(Ilex cornuta 'E.A. McIlhenny')

'E.A. McIlhenny' is another female Chinese holly that originated from a hedge planted at Jungle Gardens. Selected in 1957, it was named after the founder of Jungle Gardens. This plant forms a large shrub that is semi-upright in form. Leaves are a glossy dark green and may reach 3 inches long and 1½ inches wide. The number of spines may vary, with many leaves having five. The fruit, in abundant clusters, is red and may be 7/16 inch in diameter.

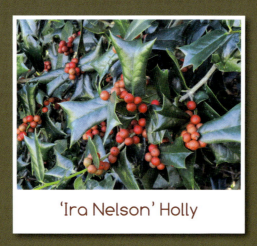

'Ira Nelson' Holly
(*Ilex cornuta* 'Ira Nelson')

'Jungle Gardens'
(*Ilex cornuta* 'Jungle Gardens')

Another female 1957 Jungle Gardens selection, this holly was named for a prominent Louisiana horticulturist. This holly is a large, upright shrub with a loose habit. Leaves are dark green and have a contrasting light-yellow line along the margins. The leaves are 2⅜ inches long by 1⅜ to 2⅜ inches wide. Margins may have a varying number of spines, but the terminal spine is typically oriented strongly downward. Fruit is bright red and may reach ½ inch in diameter.

'Jungle Gardens' is a female Chinese holly selected by E. McIlhenny in the late 1940s from a hedge at Jungle Garde 'Jungle Gardens' is a large shrub, but it is more compact t the other Jungle Garden selections discussed here. Leav are dark green and 1⅝ to 2⅛ inches long and 1 to 1¾ inch wide with one to five spines. Fruit is ¼ inch diameter and

D'Or Holly
(*Ilex cornuta* 'D'Or)

'D'Or' is a female, yellow-fruited Chinese holly that may reach 18 feet tall. Originating in Georgia in the 1950s, this holly has dark green leaves that are 2 to 2¾ inches long and 1 to 1⅝ inches long. Leaves typically only have a terminal spine. Fruits may reach ½ inch in diameter and persist into spring.

O'Spring Holly
(*Ilex cornuta* 'O'Spring')

'O'Spring' (or 'O. Spring' for its namesake Otto Spring) is a male Chinese holly introduced by an Alabama nursery in the late 1950s. This holly stands out for its variegated leaves rather than fruit and can be used as a specimen in the landscape. The leaves are distinctly mottled with sunny yellow and traditional green splotches. Leaves tend to have one to four spines per side and are 2 to 4 inches long and ¾ to 1⅜ inches wide. The mature plant may reach 10 feet tall and will tolerate light shade. It has very rarely been reported to produce red fruit or branches with solid yellow leaves.

Lusterleaf Holly
(Ilex latifolia)

Lusterleaf holly is a large evergreen tree that is typically pyramidal in shape and may reach 60 feet in the wild. Leaves are dark green and large with coarse teeth, reaching 4 to 6½ inches long and 1½ to 4 inches wide. The fruit are dull red and ⅓ inch in diameter. This plant has been described as similar in texture to southern magnolia without the messy leaf litter.

Emily Bruner Holly
'Emily Bruner' *(Ilex cornuta* 'Burfordii' x *Ilex latifolia)*

This female holly originated in Tennessee in the 1960s and was released in 1972. 'Emily Bruner' is a hybrid between 'Burfordii' and lusterleaf holly. The leaves are dark green and 2¾ to 4⅜ inches long and 1⅝ to 2⅛ inches wide. Leaves have 10 to 13 spines along each margin. This plant grows into a small tree reaching 20 to 30 feet tall with a pyramidal shape. Fruit is red and 5⁄16 inch in diameter.

Mississippi Yaupon Releases

Yaupon Holly

(Ilex vomitoria)

Yaupon holly is an evergreen native to Mississippi. Plants can range in size from dwarf shrubs to small trees, and numerous cultivars are available. Their variability allows them to find a home in most landscapes, functioning as foundation plantings, screens, hedges, specimens, espaliers, or topiaries. Mature plants may reach 30 feet tall. Leaves tend to be small with shallow serrations, and color can vary in shades of green with reddish or bluish tones. Most fruit are 1⁄16 to 5⁄16 inch in diameter and glossy red. However, several yellow-fruited cultivars are available, including one called 'Wiggins', named after the Stone County town. It was discovered and released by the same Alabama nurseryman who released 'O'Spring'. Both male and female cultivars are available.

Kathy Ann Yaupon
(Ilex vomitoria 'Kathy Ann')

'Kathy Ann' was discovered in Stone County, Mississippi. Released in 1985, the holly was named by nurseryman Dan Batson in honor of his wife. This holly's leaves are dark green and ¾ to ⅞ inch long and ⅝ to 9⁄16 inch wide. Fruit is abundant and bright red in singles or small clusters. 'Kathy Ann' has an upright habit and may reach 10 to 15 feet tall.

Scarlet's Peak Yaupon
(Ilex vomitoria 'Scarlet's Peak')

Discovered by the same nursery that released 'Kathy Ann', 'Scarlet's Peak' was released in 2008. This holly has a very narrow shape—only around 3 feet wide and reaching 20 feet tall. Dark-green leaves contrast nicely with bright-red fruit during the winter.

Mary Nell Holly
'Mary Nell' [(*Ilex cornuta* 'Burfordii' x *Ilex pernyi* 'Red Delight') x *Ilex latifolia*]

This holly originated in Alabama in 1961 and was selected and named in 1981. Leaves are dark green and may reach 3½ inches long and 1¾ inches wide. The leaf margins feature 8 to 10 very uniform spines per side. The abundant fruit is red and 5⁄16 to ⅜ inch in diameter. Growth habit is pyramidal and upright, and the plant responds well to pruning.

Foster's #2, Foster's Holly
(*Ilex* x *attenuata* 'Fosteri')

Hollies in this group are actually interspecific hybrids between *Ilex cassine* and *Ilex opaca*. 'Fosteri' hollies were selected in Alabama, with #2 being the most common. Leaves are small and dark green with spines along the margins. Growth habit is pyramidal, and plants may reach 20 to 30 feet. Foster's holly consistently bears small, red fruit.

Savannah Holly
(*Ilex* x *attenuata* 'Savannah')

Savannah holly comes from the same interspecific hybrids as 'Foster's', but the leaves are much larger and lighter green. The leaves do have small spines and look similar to American holly. 'Savannah' holly has a plentiful crop of ⅓-inch red berries in the fall. This plant can reach 30 feet tall.

Nellie R. Stevens Holly
(*Ilex cornuta* x *Ilex aquifolium*)

This selection dates to 1900. 'Nellie R. Stevens' has dark green leaves that are 2¾ to 3½ inches long and 1³⁄16 to 2⅜ inches wide. Leaf margins may have two or three spines per side. This holly forms a large shrub or small tree reaching 15 to 25 feet tall. Fruit is red and may reach ⅓ inch in diameter. This holly does fruit heavily, but it does not last as long as some of the other choices.

Little Bethlehem

Fireplace mantels provide the room with a focal point and, therefore, can be the perfect location for a nativity, the most important decoration in some families. Nativities were developed in Italy, and the picturesque Via San Gregorio Armeno alleyway in Naples, where countless sets are sold, is a UNESCO World Heritage Site.

The nativity scene and containers in this image were Mississippi-made by designer and craftsman David Mills. In homage to the stable where Jesus was born, the floral materials in this composition are humble and simply arranged, though they were carefully placed.

This floral container has wooden skewers placed into pre-drilled holes in a log cross-section. We used rubber bands to hold water tubes in place and inserted *Helleborus niger* (Christmas rose) stems. With their deep green leaves, these lime flowers are known to bloom when no other flowers are able, in the winter cold.

Red Hollies

These hollies were selected in the 1980s at a nursery in Pearl River County from seedlings of 'Mary Nell'. The leaves have distinctive spines, and new growth is reddish.

Oakland™ (*Ilex* x 'Magland')

Oakland has leaves reminiscent of oak leaves with heavy spines, although the spines are not particularly sharp compared to some other hollies. This holly has a pyramidal growth habit and can reach 15 to 20 feet tall and almost as wide. Red berries tend to be late in the season.

Robin™ (*Ilex* x 'Conin')

Robin has leaves that are moderately spined, similar to those of 'Nellie R. Stevens'. This holly has a pyramidal growth habit and matures at around 15 to 20 feet tall and 12 to 15 feet wide. Robin produces bright red berries in the fall. New foliage emerges as maroon-red in the spring.

Christmas Rose
(*Helleborus niger*)

Christmas rose, *Helleborus niger*, is a low-growing, evergreen, herbaceous perennial that blooms beginning in the winter and into the early spring. Christmas roses prefer moist, shaded areas of the landscape, and morning sunlight may encourage plants to produce more flowers than those grown entirely in the shade. Christmas roses offer a range of colors from white or light pink to intense purple. Flowers may last up to 3 months from the start of bloom. Blooms frequently face downward, so plant them in containers to get a better view of the flowers. Some new varieties produce upright flowers.

Christmas rose grows in clumps about 2 feet wide by 2 feet tall. Cutting them back before bloom will both remove any damaged foliage and improve flowering. Christmas rose will often produce seedlings that can be transplanted. Lenten rose, *Helleborus orientalis*, is similar in its growth habit, but as is suggested by its name, blooms in February and March.

Elaeagnus Wreath

Many people think of Elaeagnus as a fencerow plant. When planted 10 feet apart or less, the shrubs grow into a seemingly impermeable fence in as little as 10 years. These plants send long, leggy, flexible sprouts well above the leafy mass of the plant's body. These branches can be formed into circles without the need for additional wreath bases or forms. We used about 10 Elaeagnus branches to form this wreath. It will dry in place and can be used indefinitely. You can also use the dried version as the base for a wreath decorated with cones, artificial fruit, and natural-toned ribbons. In its fresh state, it conveys spontaneity and allows creative florists to imagine the possibilities.

Thorny Elaeagnus
(*Elaeagnus pungens*)

With wavy, dark green evergreen leaves contrasting with silvery undersides, this plant has truly distinctive foliage. Its leaves may reach 2 to 4 inches long and 1¼ to 1¾ inches wide. It is an incredibly durable landscape plant, and it has been used for mass plantings, hedges, screens, and highway medians. Note that it suckers and can be difficult to contain in a landscape. It can easily reach 10 to 15 feet tall with a similar width, and it can give the appearance of climbing into trees or onto other landscape features.

Be careful when handling or harvesting thorny elaeagnus because it does produce 2- to 3-inch-long thorns. It has fragrant, small, tubular flowers in the fall. Long branches make this a versatile design component that can easily be incorporated into floral decorations. Selections are available with yellow to cream variegation, and some have bright silver leaf undersides.

Pink Princettia® Wreath

All the materials in this wreath were grown in Mississippi. We used a fresh floral foam wreath as the base and added the greenery, keeping an eye toward covering the outer and inner edges of the foam ring. A technique to make "greening" the base more efficient is to roll aspidistra leaves (*Aspidistra elatior*) so that their stemlike petioles pierce through the leaf and into the foam. In this way, they cover the floral foam but do not add too much bulk.

For this design, we harvested J'Adore Pink Princettia® blooms from a single plant and immediately placed them in fresh flower food solution. These flowers are members of the Euphorbiaceae family.

We cut our stems from the plant to the exact length needed for the design so that the stems did not continue to "bleed" sap. While the flowers were taking up water, we moistened the wreath frame and then overwrapped it with waterproof tape, leaving 6-inch gaps to receive flowers and greenery. This extra step ensures that the foam segments do not detach from the papier-mâché base.

After 1 hour, we arranged the flowers into the wet foam, then gave the wreath a few minutes to drip dry before hanging. This same design makes a stunning table arrangement with candles in its center.

Materials

- Floral foam wreath form, 22- or 24-inch diameter
- Waterproof tape
- Aspidistra
- Boxwood
- Florida anise
- Leyland cypress
- Poinsettia

Floral Design Careers

Many jobs are available, both full and part-time, in floral design.
- Event and wedding florist
- Florist shop manager
- Floristry teacher
- Freelance floral designer
- Product developer
- Sales specialist
- Specialty florist (casinos, cinemas, cruise ships, hotels, museums, private estates)
- Wholesale floral sales and designer

Magnolia Mantel

Regal, Southern, timeless. These words describe the beauty of cut magnolia foliage in floral designs. Magnolia leaves' thick and waxy cuticle layer provides just enough glimmer for decoration, both inside and out. A commercial cut-foliage farmer made this wreath using a clamp-type wreath ring. This manually powered machine allows farmers to produce numerous wreaths for sales on the farm or through retail florists and nurseries.

When purchasing magnolia wreaths and garlands, look for bright green, crisp leaves. Keep your wreath and garland in a plastic bag in the refrigerator until you're ready to work with them. Be sure to poke a few holes in the bag to allow air transfer and lessen the chance for mold growth.

Living decorations like these will lose moisture over time. You can expect them to remain in their fresh state for about a week, give or take a few days. We tend to expect our fresh decorations to remain crisp and fresh much longer than is possible. There are sprays and coatings on the market that are designed to keep flowers fresher, but their effect is measured in hours, not days or weeks. The closer the display to heat sources or warm spaces (fireplaces, ceilings, strong sunlight), the faster the foliage will dry.

One option is to purchase two or more magnolia wreaths and garlands, storing the extra in the refrigerator while the other is on display. You can refresh the display before an event.

Many designers like the look of dried magnolias, even saving their wreaths and adding dried flowers to the design for year-round display. You can spray paint magnolia in either its fresh or dried state with good effect, using gold or other colors.

It is important to understand how plant materials behave in the design environment. Ask yourself these questions:

- What is the necessary effect of the design?
- When does it need to look its best?
- For how long?
- How much time can I devote to decoration maintenance/ replacement?

Given these few constraints, magnolia foliage garlands and wreaths are some of the most beautiful decorations imaginable from the Southern landscape.

Southern Magnolias

As both the state tree and flower of Mississippi, the southern magnolia (*Magnolia grandiflora*) is a prized component of many landscapes. These trees are native to the entire Southeast from Maryland to Florida and west to Texas. Southern magnolias may reach 80 feet tall and can be grown in a variety of environmental conditions, although they prefer acidic and moist but well-drained soils. Known for their large and fragrant white flowers, improved southern magnolia selections in the landscape may flower from early spring until frost.

The evergreen foliage of southern magnolias provides texture and contrast to the garden terrain. The leaves are large, glossy, and long-lasting with dark green upper surfaces and often brown, fuzzy undersides. These characteristics make southern magnolia an excellent source of greenery for seasonal decorations. Southern magnolias are considered a staple of Colonial Williamsburg Christmas decorations.

Depending on the size of the landscape, southern magnolias can be used as specimen plants, grown in hedges, or planted in small groupings. Larger southern magnolias such as 'D.D. Blanchard', 'Bracken's Brown Beauty', and 'Claudia Wannamaker' make excellent specimen trees in the landscape. Smaller southern magnolias such as 'Little Gem', 'Teddy Bear', and 'Alta' can be used as small specimen trees or grown in a line as a hedge. Because southern magnolias can be messy as they drop some leaves, many people choose to leave them with limbs reaching the ground and simply rake the fallen leaves under the canopy.

'D.D. Blanchard'
This southern magnolia selection has been around since the 1940s and originated in North Carolina. 'D.D. Blanchard' has incredibly dark green leaves accented by heavy, orange-brown fuzz on their undersides. Flowers can be 8 inches wide. This plant will mature into a pyramidal tree that can exceed 50 feet tall.

'Bracken's Brown Beauty'
This southern magnolia selection was made in South Carolina in the late 1960s and features leaves that are around 6 inches long with wavy margins and brown

D.D. Blanchard

D.D. Blanchard

Claudia Wannamaker

Little Gem

fuzz underneath. Although selected in the South, 'Bracken's Brown Beauty' has a reputation as one of the most cold-hardy magnolias available. This tree tends to have a dense, full canopy, reaching 30 to 50 feet tall. Flowers are 5 to 6 inches in diameter. This selection does not drop as many leaves, making it cleaner in the home landscape. This is one of the most popular southern magnolias.

'Claudia Wannamaker'
Another South Carolina introduction, 'Claudia Wannamaker' has dark green foliage. Its underside fuzz is less pronounced than that of 'D.D. Blanchard' and 'Bracken's Brown Beauty'. This selection flowers well even when young. 'Claudia Wannamaker' matures into a large, broadly pyramidal tree that may exceed 50 feet tall. This tree is also very common in nurseries and garden centers.

'Little Gem'
This selection was made in North Carolina in the 1950s. It was originally marketed as a dwarf southern magnolia, but mature plantings have reached 30 feet. It does tend to be multi-stemmed, which makes it an excellent choice for hedges. 'Little Gem' has 4-inch leaves and 3- to 4-inch-diameter flowers that fully open to around 6 inches. The undersides of the leaves have a heavy brown fuzz. Although the flowers are small, this plant blooms heavily throughout the growing season until frost. This selection is incredibly popular in landscapes of all sizes.

'Teddy Bear'
This selection, sometimes known as 'Southern Charm', was selected in South Carolina in 1985. It has a narrow, pyramidal shape with very dense foliage. The leaves are 5 to 8 inches long and tend to be cupped with heavy, brown fuzz on the undersides that makes them look like a teddy bear's ears. 'Teddy Bear' has larger flowers than 'Little Gem', but it flowers less heavily. This semi-dwarf tree matures at less than 30 feet tall and 20 feet wide, making it suitable for many landscapes.

Teddy Bear

Alta

'Alta'
'Alta' was discovered at a nursery in Georgia in 1993. This is a very upright southern magnolia with dark green leaves and moderate fuzz on the undersides. The leaves are long and narrow, 6 to 8 inches long and 1½ to 2½ inches wide. 'Alta' tends to be smaller than 'Little Gem' and 'Teddy Bear' but features large flowers that can reach 8 to 10 inches in diameter. 'Alta' brings the classic southern magnolia look to smaller landscapes.

Welcome, Christmas!

Red ribbon bows on lampposts and wreaths,
with long streamers that flutter in the breeze.
Sunny days, cool nights.
Everything's more beautiful with Christmastime lights.

The Two Sisters: Camellia and Rosemary

Ring a doorway with the welcoming signs of Christmas using festive greenery and red-velvet bows. Southern gardens can offer the materials necessary to create this cheery look. We were inspired by the textural contrast of smooth, shiny camellia leaves and fir-like rosemary branches.

We made a long garland, then cut it in half. We re-attached the pieces so that the foliage flowed downward from the central attachment just above the door. As the foliage dries in place, the downward lines of the individual branches keep a neater appearance.

Next, we wired heavily berried boughs of holly (*Ilex cornuta* 'Jungle Gardens') in place, then we added red-velvet bows—the undisputed classics of Christmas floral design. Cap off the front door with a coordinating wreath and welcome family and friends to your home with your picture-postcard front door!

Rosemary
(*Rosmarinus officinalis*)

Rosemary is commonly grown as an herb, but there are numerous ways to integrate it into the landscape. It is consistently hardy across Mississippi. Rosemary is an evergreen shrub that may reach 2 to 4 feet tall and wide in the landscape. Commonly seen as a rangy perennial in mixed beds, it can be pruned into more formal shapes. It lends itself well to both mixed and individual planters, and it is often trimmed into a cone, decorated with red ribbon, and sold during the holiday season. It can be integrated into seasonal decorations

as both a whole plant and as cut foliage. It can be perennial, and color is usually deeper during the winter months. The plant is highly fragrant. Numerous cultivars are available, but it is common to see it simply sold as "rosemary."

Evergreens on a Straw Wreath

Wreaths are symbols of everlasting life. Intrinsic to their design, they are the epitome of visual motion. Their line is dynamic and constantly changing.

Creating your own fresh, green wreath is a fun and calming activity during the hustle of the holiday season. In our view, the prettiest wreaths are those using just the elements of nature—fresh, natural foliage. We opted for a straw base rather than wire or plastic foam.

They are easy to work with and biodegradable, and they allow you to create a full, abundant wreath. It is quite possible to create your own natural wreath base using straw or other dried grass and paddle wire.

1. Assemble a variety of evergreens for this design. The only other materials necessary for this project are wire greening pins, sold by floral and craft outlets.

2. Gather a small bunch of evergreens and pin them to the interior of the wreath ring.

3. Add the next bunch to the outer surface of the wreath.

4. Add a third bunch to the wreath's top surface. Leave the back plain if the wreath is to be displayed on a door or wall.

5. You may want to cover the back of the wreath with more greenery if you plan to hang it in a window.

6. Continue this process, working in one direction to achieve a pleasing flow of materials.

7. Display your wreath. Once family and friends see them, they will want to "put in an order," so plan to make more than one!

Pine Cone Wreath

Pine trees are in great abundance throughout the Southeast. Turn a fresh eye to their design use for the fall and winter season by creating a lavish wreath with pine cones. Our design uses only slash pine (*Pinus elliottii*) cones, but you can use others alone or in mixes for beautiful effects. Each cone is individually wired to a reinforced wire wreath form. The cost of making this wreath is negligible, but it does take some time to gather and wire the pine cones.

You can make a design like this over a few days, but it is easier to think of this design construction as something that takes months to create. Floral design does not need to be a rushed activity. It can be a way of keeping in tune with nature, and a single design can take two or more seasons to create. This kind of natural arrangement reflects our beautiful native landscape.

Children may enjoy helping to create a design like this. Every trip to the wood's edge can yield a bag of cones, and, by Thanksgiving, you will have enough to make a wreath that echoes many happy memories.

Collect pine cones throughout the year and store them in a dry place until you're ready to use them. We did not use any pesticides on our cones. Once the design was finished, we lacquered it with wood-toned aerosol stain.

Evergreen Garland

Garland is one of the oldest floral design forms on record. It was used to adorn buildings and interior dwellings of the ancient Romans and Greeks. Little wonder that this classic has stood the test of time.

Every floral enthusiast should make garlands. Evergreens, berries, and cones are traditional, but you can make garlands from numerous materials. Try using fresh flowers, dried flowers, and fruit to create visually stunning work.

For this design, you need a paddle of green wire (#22 or #24 gauge) and strong rope. You can find the wire at floral supply and craft stores. Cut wire does not work as well for this project because you need a continuous length for consistent wrapping. We selected rappelling rope because of its strength, camouflage colors, and availability at a local hardware store.

Begin by winding the wire around the end of the rope, attaching it firmly. We started off by bending the wire into an L shape so that the short end of the wire could be wrapped in with the rope.

Gather a selection of evergreens for your project. You can purchase foliage, use locally grown greenery, or combine the two. We opted for Mississippi-grown foliage and even added some lichen-covered crape myrtle stems. Recut the evergreen stems and place them in water for a minimum of 1 hour to ensure that they take up the maximum amount of water. If you have flower food, mix that into the water first because it promotes water uptake. After the foliage has taken up water, cut it to 6- to 10-inch lengths.

Add foliage, berries, and twigs to the rope in bunches, then wind the wire around the combination of rope and stems. Continue this process, alternating foliage types if you are using a mix. For a garland with a fuller appearance, add greenery on all sides so that the rope forms a central core.

When you have reached the desired length, bring one end of the wire into a loop on one side of the rope, extending the rest of the wire on the right side.

Grasping the left and right ends, twist them around each other to secure the wire in place.

Cut the twisted wire, fork the ends in place, and press the cut ends into the network of stems and rope. This will help keep the sharp wires from scratching surfaces or fingers. Cut away the extra rope. Form the rope into a loop and wire it in place.

Once completed, you can store the finished garland in a plastic bag in the refrigerator (remember to poke holes in the bag). Anti-transpirant sprays are available, but they add hours to the design's life, not days or weeks. Heat and being indoors shorten the garland's freshness, but many evergreens dry beautifully, taking on an antique texture and color. Capitalize on this effect by decorating with pine cones, dried flowers, and ribbon in subtle colors.

How to Make a Bow

It is handy to know how to make a symmetrical bow. Bows can help to repeat a color or pattern in your holiday decorations, with uses on stairways, wreaths, and trees. You can also decorate gifts and make them special year-round.

Some holiday ribbons are single-faced, meaning that they are decorative on only one side. With this type of ribbon, you will need to twist the ribbon each time you make a loop to keep the decorated side visible.

It takes about 4 yards of #40 (about 3 inches wide) ribbon to create a bow with streamers.

Florist wire and chenille stems (craft pipe cleaners) can be used to hold a bow together. Take care to avoid wire that may scratch wood surfaces. Paper-covered wire is a handy floral design mechanic for this purpose.

When adding a bow to a gift, do not use wire to hold it together because it could scratch someone during handling. Simply substitute ribbon to hold the bow together. Add the ribbon tie to the package first so that, after you make the bow, you can simply bind it in place.

1. You will need a bolt of ribbon, some florist wire (approximately #24 gauge), and a pair of sharp scissors.

2. Unroll a few yards of the ribbon and gather it in your hand, making a loop. Note that we left a streamer or tail. During construction, always keep this streamer at the back of the bow and don't handle or manipulate it until the bow is completed.

3. Pinch the ribbon together between your index finger and thumb. Give the extra ribbon, not including the original streamer, a half-twist to the right. This will expose the nondecorative side of the ribbon.

4. Bring the second ribbon loop to the pinch point. Now, the decorative side of the ribbon will be showing again.

5. At this part of the process, you will have two loops, each displaying the decorative side of the ribbon. The emerging design should resemble a bow tie.

6. Continue the process of making a loop, gathering it at the binding point, then half-twisting the ribbon to the right. Alternate this process on both sides of the binding point so that there are four loops on the left and four loops on the right. Continue to check your work, making sure the decorative side of the ribbon is on display.

7. Next, make a loop to disguise the binding wire. Make the loop over your thumb, then hold it under your thumb. Again, think of this loop as a cover for the nondecorative wire.

8. This image shows the side of the bow in progress. Note that the center loop is small and that the ribbon attached to the bolt flies away from it. This extra ribbon will become the second streamer.

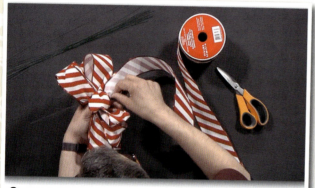

9. Insert the wire through the center loop on top of the bow.

10. Bring the wire around the backside of the bow. Keep the arms of the wire at even lengths. Pull the wire taut.

11. Twist the wire arms together to create a tight bind.

12. Using your shears, trim the ribbon so that it is nearly even with the first streamer.

13. Open the loops to create a symmetrical, fluffed appearance.

14. Pull the streamers in place so that they flow downward.

Cardinals in Evergreen Planter

A flock of bright red cardinals beckon the winter season! Stay-in-place clips keep birds on the bough for the season, but you'll need to wire the birds in place for off-the-porch displays.

Instead of artificial greenery this year, check out the selection of potted plants at your local garden center. After the holidays, you can extend the life of your live evergreens by planting them in the home landscape. Transplanting them before the warm days of mid- to late spring gives the plants time to acclimate and allows their roots to take up abundant winter and spring rains.

The plants shown here are Leyland cypress (*Cupressus × leylandii*) with underplantings of *Asparagus densiflorus* (asparagus fern) and *Ardisia crenata*. Consult with your local nursery retailer for selections that will be best for porch and patio displays.

Bypass the need to plug in electric lights every night by using solar lights. During the daytime, mini solar panels take in light energy and, even with short, gloomy days, power the miniature lights for several hours.

Holiday Decorating Checklist

- Fresh magnolia or evergreen wreath
- Evergreen plants
- Poinsettias, holiday plants
- Cut evergreen boughs
- Supplies: chicken wire, floral foam, paper-covered wire, ribbon, waterproof tape, wooden picks

The Living Room

Dried Floral Christmas Tree

The Christmas tree is a beloved symbol of the season. Our memories are filled with them because they are the focal point of all home holiday decorations. We fill their branches with ornaments and lights and delight in their beauty both day and night. As horticulturists, we feel the most beautiful tree "ornaments" are flowers! Imagine your Christmas tree filled with locally grown flowers.

This fir tree is illuminated with white lights, then lavished with the subdued, romantic colors of dried flowers. We grew our flowers in the summer at the South Mississippi Branch Experiment Station in Poplarville and harvested them at maturity, as the season commenced. We rubber-banded together bunches of five, ten, or twenty stems, depending on size, and then hung them upside down on clothesline to dry in a barn. After about 2 weeks of drying time in the late-summer heat, we gently removed them from the barn and stored them in the dark, in boxes, to protect them from sunlight and insects.

The dried flowers decorating our tree:

- *Ammobium alatum* — Winged everlasting
- *Celosia crestata* — Cockscomb
- *Consolida ajacis* — Larkspur
- *Gomphrena globose* — Globe amaranth
- *Helianthus annuus* — Sunflower
- *Hydrangea paniculate* — Panicle hydrangea
- *Lavandula angustifolia* — 'Ellagance' lavender
- *Triticum aestivum* — Wheat
- *Achillea filipendulina* — Yarrow

Dried Floral Stairway Nosegays

A French-style handtied nosegay of dried flowers can be the starting point for numerous design applications beyond flowers to carry. We opted out of using ribbon and, instead, used dried flowers to provide a nostalgic focal point where garland is caught on the stairway railing. Try using lavender in the mix for a soft, calming fragrance while on your way up or down the stairs.

Camellia shrubs provide a durable, long-lasting foliage that is excellent for garlands. Old homesteads and farms often have large Japonica camellia shrubs that have never been pruned. Use this foliage for long-lasting centerpieces or other fresh floral designs.

Globe amaranth
(*Gomphrena globosa*)

Globe amaranth is a member of the Amaranthaceae family, which is native to the tropics of India. These flowers grow to 18 inches tall with a bushy habit. Gomphrena's round, ball-like flowers are produced at the ends of stems. Flowers are white, pink, purple, and magenta. Some newer varieties are selections of *Gomphrena haageana* or hybrids between the two species. These have a more upright growth habit and

have flowers in red tones. Gomphrena flowers consist of bracts, or modified leaves, while the true flowers are small, yellow, and trumpet shaped. Because of these long-lasting bracts, globe amaranth provides an extended show in the landscape.

You can start gomphrena from seed. Soak them in water before planting to improve their germination. Space globe amaranth 12 to 18 inches apart. It works well in mass plantings and containers. Globe amaranth prefers full sun and is moderately tolerant of drought. We like these flowers for dried arrangements because they retain their color for many months after drying. Harvest them once the blooms fully open, and hang the stems in a warm, dark, well-ventilated area. You can create designs with them after about 2 weeks of drying.

Lavender
(*Lavandula angustifolia*)

Lavender is popular in the garden as both a beautiful flower and an herb. Lavender, a member of the mint family (Lamiaceae), is a semi-evergreen, woody shrub that forms mounds 2 feet across and up to 18 inches tall. Lavender is extraordinarily aromatic and is often used in aromatherapy, either fresh or as an oil. Flowers are formed on slender spikes 8 to 12 inches above the canopy. Flowers are clustered on the ends of spikes. While blue or purple is most common, varieties with white or pink flowers are available.

Lavender grows best in full sun and slightly sandy and alkaline soils. Wet soils can lead to decline. Lavender can be direct-seeded or transplanted. Every third year in early spring, prune clumps of lavender back to around 8 inches. Pruning and deadheading in late summer will promote reblooming. Dried flowers make an excellent potpourri.

Japanese Camellia
(*Camellia japonica*)

Japanese camellias are a classic in many Southern gardens. The foliage is evergreen, providing options for using this large shrub/small tree as a hedge or screen, in mixed plantings, or as a specimen in the landscape.

Some shade is preferable. Mature size may be 20 to 25 feet tall and 6 to 10 feet wide. The leaves are 2 to 4 inches long and ovate to elliptical. Leaves are thick and waxy, making them a nice foliage option for floral designs.

Japanese camellias provide color in the landscape at a time when most other plants are moving toward dormancy. If you select appropriate cultivars, camellias can provide flowers for the landscape and decorations from October through April. Flower colors include white, pink, red, and numerous variegated combinations. Flowers may be single or double and may reach up to 6 inches in diameter. Flowers are dropped as complete blooms rather than individual petals.

Camellia shows are common in the South, and buds may be "gibbed" to produce early and large flowers. Gibbing involves removing the vegetative bud adjacent to the desired flower bud. A drop of gibberellic acid is placed in the bud cup of the vegetative bud. September is a common time for this treatment. Freezes may damage the flowers, and severe cold can damage the plants.

Sasanqua Camellia
(*Camellia sasanqua*)

Like its showier cousin, the sasanqua camellia is a staple in many Southern gardens. The foliage is still evergreen, but the overall habit of the plant is less formal and more irregular than Japanese camellia. Sasanquas can be used for a less formal look in decorations. Sasanquas typically reach 6 to 15 feet tall. Leaves are 1½ to 3 inches long and a third to half as wide. They are obovate to oval.

These plants start flowering in September and may continue through December or later. While the flowers are smaller than those of the Japanese camellia, sasanquas come in a similar range of colors and may also be single or double. Petals are shed individually, and the area underneath the plants may resemble a floral carpet when petal drop occurs. Sasanquas are generally less cold hardy than Japanese camellias.

Boxwood Topiary

Boxwood topiary trees are fun to make and require just a few materials to create. We arranged ours in fresh flower foam so that it would remain crisp and green for the season. If watered a few times a week, boxwood topiaries will last into the new year.

To care for this design, take it to the sink and allow water to drip on the top. The driest part of the floral foam is at the top, so give special attention to hydrating this portion first. Allow the tree to drip dry, and leave some water in its container. If you want to take an extra step to keep the tree fresh longer, place it on the porch or in an unheated garage overnight. This cold period "refrigerates" the green design when there is no one to enjoy it and can extend its fresh display time by weeks. Keep the design out of direct sunlight and away from heat sources.

We added maroon hypericum berries and pinkish-red miniature carnations to our tree for color. The possibilities for decorating your version are endless if you consider dried flowers, pods, permanent floral materials, or other fresh flowers.

Madonna and Child

White is a dominant color in this arrangement, featured in the oriental lilies and given depth by the bright-red holly berries and miniature carnations. The combination of red, green, and white at Christmas symbolizes purity, sacrifice, and everlasting life. An arrangement like this makes a thoughtful gift, especially when the meanings of the colors are conveyed.

Commercial growers often produce oriental lilies for holiday sales. Purchase these in bud form and enjoy the slow unfurling of their petals and sepals. Remember to remove each flower's anthers as they begin to open to avoid pollen staining.

Contemporary vase arrangements in clear glass make their way into the holiday season easily when you vary the colors and types of flowers used. Choose a bunch of mixed flowers, and arrange them with evergreen clippings from the landscape. These boutique-style designs are lovely when displayed beneath a lamp's pool of light.

Remember the traditional proportion for vase arrangements is to make the design one and a half to two times the height of the container. The floral materials are more dominant in size than the vase, creating the look of abundance without appearing top-heavy.

An important part of this design is keeping the water clear and clean. Doing so greatly lengthens the display life of the flowers. Floral designers should discard the vase water immediately after designing, replacing it with newly mixed fresh flower food solution. Organic (soil or leaf) debris quickly collects in the vase during the design process. This dirty solution harbors microbes that clog the water-conducting vessels of cut stems.

The best practice for commercial florists is to make the design in one vase, then transfer it to an identical vase with clean, fresh flower food solution. This will keep the design as fresh as it can be, presented in clean water.

Evergreen Swag

Historically, expert wood carvers created relief decoration in the interiors of wealthy estate owners. Such sculptures reached an apex in the work of

18th century Anglo-Dutch artist Grinling Gibbons (1648–1721). Taking a cue from his work, we created a formal adornment for a wall sconce using fresh foliage and dried materials. A floral foam cage provides a temporary water source to keep greenery fresh.

We used greenery purchased from a florist along with some materials from nearby gardens. The focal area of the design is encrusted with lotus pods (water lily fruit), pine cones, cinnamon sticks, and dried citrus slices. Note that the dried elements as well as the fresh greens cascade downward, emphasizing the elegant pendant line. Even when dry, this arrangement remains a tasteful decoration. Keep this idea in mind for church or clubhouse decorations.

Mixed Evergreen Topiary

Do you have space for a design where the proportion of the arrangement is lifted high above the tabletop? You may find inspiration in this rounded, spreading topiary form made from Mississippi-grown cut evergreens.

Though the design is massive, it is light in appearance because we can see through the branches holding the arrangement in place. We grew corkscrew willow (*Salix matsudana* 'Tortuosa') for about 2 years, then pruned the plants in December after their leaves naturally fell from the stems. New shoots arise in the spring and grow for future harvests.

We arranged the fresh foliage in floral foam and added an audacious red bow to jazz up the scene. We recycled the container from the stacked pumpkin design for a fall buffet, burnishing it with walnut varnish spray paint and a few dabs of 24 karat gold. When using rugged containers, take the time to add felt feet to the base to avoid scratching glass and wood surfaces.

Bed, Bath, and Kitchen

Aromatherapy: Eucalyptus and Orange Garland

Holiday decorations can do much more than just look beautiful. We created a garland that is not only pretty, but also provides a calming and rejuvenating fragrance. What better place for an aromatherapy design but the main bath?

You can create your own garland from commercially grown, fresh eucalyptus. Our roping is made from multiple eucalyptus varieties mixed with green hypericum berries and dried orange slices. Dried oranges are available in small and large quantities through craft supply sources. If you plan on using them for multiple designs like those shown in this book, consider purchasing a food dehydrator, some of which are available for under $50.

Make a garland of dried orange slices by piercing brown, paper-covered wire into each slice and then twisting it to hold the slices in place. Add the lightweight orange garland to the heavier, green garland so the orange slices will not be obscured behind the greenery. These little orange garlands make great tree decorations, too. Dried oranges keep their refreshing appearance indoors but not so much outdoors, where rain and strong sunlight damage them.

The fragrance from these materials is light and soothing. It creates the perfect environment to prepare for holiday festivities!

Tutsan
(*Hypericum androsaemum*)

The hypericum commonly grown for its fruit that is used in floral design is not as common in the United States as other species. However, interest is increasing, and new releases are being made from several large plant-introduction programs. The fruit can be red to almost black, different shades of pink, or white, and it will last for several weeks when cut. It can grow 2 to 3 feet tall and has a reputation for being weedy in European gardens and invasive in Australia. It is shade tolerant. We do not know if the new releases will be persistent in the Deep South heat and humidity.

Red-Violet Flourish

Lichen-covered branches provide structure, both visual and actual, in tall vases for fresh floral design. In the South, it is possible to find tree and shrub branches with a fine growth of lichen (pronounced LY-ken). Lichen is not a fungus but a symbiosis between different organisms. It does not hurt the plant on which it is growing and is a natural part of Southern landscapes.

Designers see much beauty in lichens and lichen-covered branches because of their color, pattern, and texture. Their rugged appearance is the perfect contrast to elegant, smooth textures. Combine these branches with stems of lilies, roses, orchids, or, as we did, gladioli (glads).

Glads bloom in the summer in Southern gardens, but we found ours at a flower market. The red-violet color is reminiscent of the candles used in Advent wreaths. Violet is the color of kings, so in liturgical floral design, it represents welcoming the arrival of the King Jesus. Our vase was manufactured by McCarty Pottery of Merigold, Mississippi.

Poinsettia Garden

Consider simplifying holiday decorating by skipping small details and adopting bold designs this year. Often, one large arrangement provides better impact

than several smaller ones. This is a technique used by the best florists, and a big, showy display does not have to be expensive. Garden centers carry poinsettias from late November onward, often selling them for just a few dollars per pot. At the end of the season, you can discard the plants in the compost pile, knowing that they will replenish the following year's garden soil.

When shopping at off-price department stores, antique malls, or other home décor outlets, be on the lookout for large planters or containers that will hold a collection of poinsettia plants, like the ceramic container shown on the next page. Using a durable, waterproof container makes caring for this design nearly effortless. Just place the grow pots in the larger container, arranging the plants from high to low, back to front.

A collection of poinsettias, a wreath on the door, and a Christmas tree are all you need to make a house a home during the holidays!

Maintaining this poinsettia garden is easy. Display the plants in bright, indirect light. Water the individual pots within the container when the soil feels dry to the touch, taking care not to over- or under-water. One method that may work for your plants is to add about ½ inch of water to the waterproof, decorative container, allowing the plants to slowly take up the water. After about a week, repeat the process.

Poinsettia (*Euphorbia pulcherrima*) varieties
Top left: 'Christmas Mouse'
Top right: 'Christmas Rose'
Bottom left: 'Burning Ember'
Bottom right: Princettia Red®

Colonial Lantern

The warm glow from holiday candlelight is enhanced when displayed on a bed of greenery. This design combines all the favorite cut greens used by Southern floral design enthusiasts. We have a wealth of beautiful and unusual leaves and branches just outside the door that look incredible in floral design!

There is nothing like the golden glow of flickering candlelight. It provides a cozy appearance and a feeling of warmth. Families in the early 19th century and earlier dined by candlelight, often using just one to illuminate the entire room.

Lanterns are considered a decorating classic, harkening to the days before electricity. Today, they are a designer trend and can safely contain lit candles. Battery-powered and solar lights are excellent substitutes when candlelight cannot be constantly monitored for safety. Scale this design down by using a smaller lantern and a single candle.

We made this arrangement in a durable plastic tray with two blocks of fresh flower foam taped in place. We added a layer of thick plastic film cut to the footprint size of the lantern and placed it on top of the foam before taping it in place. The waterproof layer keeps the lantern from forming rust, allowing for many seasons of use. If you replicate this design, be sure to keep the foliage from extending more than 1 inch above the base of the lantern. Add water to the arrangement's container every 2 to 3 days to keep it fresh and vibrant.

We kept the design simple and pure, revealing the gentle variations of green and diverse leaf patterns. Add pine cones, fresh flowers, ribbon, and other trims to establish design theme and repetition, especially when creating and displaying multiple designs.

Cut foliage used in this arrangement:

- Atlantic white cedar
- Camellia
- Florida anise
- Holly
- Variegated Japanese pittosporum

Santolina Garlands and Wreaths

Expecting company this holiday? Imagine the excitement and surprise of guests, particularly dear grandchildren, when they settle in for "a long winter's nap" in comfy beds decorated with wreaths and garland. We chose silvery santolina (*Santolina chamaecyparissus*), also known as lavender cotton, for the footboard design shown on page 106. Native to the Mediterranean, this plant thrives in full sun with sandy, well-drained soil in Zones 6 to 9. If you can successfully grow rosemary in your garden, this plant may perform just as well.

These designs were created with fresh santolina that dries beautifully, retaining its color and form. After the holidays, you can repurpose these decorations. For example, glue pastel dried flowers into the network of santolina foliage and stems, and display the refreshed designs in the spring. See our *Dried Floral Christmas Tree* (page 92) for ideas.

A candlelight lantern design* can be perfect for:

- Church window ledges
- Fireplace hearths
- Front porch décor
- Hall tables
- Hotel/bed-and-breakfast lobbies
- Party buffet tables
- Table centerpieces

*Use artificial candles for safety.

Lavender Cotton
(*Santolina chamaecyparissus*)

Another versatile perennial with herbal uses, lavender cotton has silvery, grayish-green foliage and white pubescence. Some cultivars tend to be green. Foliage may be off-color in the winter. This plant stays small in the landscape, reaching 1 to 2 feet tall with twice the spread. It is an excellent option for mixed beds and containers or as cut foliage for decorating. It reportedly has insect-repellent properties. In the heat and humidity of the South, the plant may decline over several years and ultimately need to be replanted.

Prints and Drawings

In the tradition of old European estates, adorn the portraits of beloved ancestors with garland and boughs. This collection consists of Queen Victoria images, centered by an engraving of her daughter-in-law, Princess Alexandra of Denmark.

You can decorate images of your own "royal family" using cut evergreens. Larger frames can hold santolina garlands accented with boxwood and ribbon. Make simple garland effects by using wisps and branches of evergreens in symmetrical and asymmetrical patterns. Finding new uses for otherwise commonplace greenery and trims is invigorating!

Desk Montage

Catch up with family and friends by sending a brief note or holiday card over the miles. Your time and thoughtfulness will be appreciated. A festive desk montage can make this task even more enjoyable!

Poinsettia: Living Symbol of the Season

Poinsettias consist of colorful, leafy bracts that surround the true flowers called *cyathia*. These often shed from the plant after a few weeks, but this does not detract from the appeal of newer varieties. To keep the colorful bracts, display poinsettias in daytime temperatures between 68 and 72 degrees and nighttime around 60 degrees. Bright, indirect light keeps the bracts healthy longer. Avoid vents, space heaters, or cold wind blasts from open doors and windows.

Be sure to remove these plants from their protective sleeves and other packaging. You can keep the plant in a waterproof pot cover, but remember to drain collected water after 1 day.

Research has shown poinsettias are nontoxic, but some people may develop skin irritation from the plant's milky sap.

Poinsettia in Blue and White

Beautiful, expertly grown poinsettias such as this 'Burning Ember' deserve more than a plastic pot cover. Indeed, they are worthy of the best display containers people can create. Blue and white pottery has been produced for centuries in China, Iraq, and the Netherlands, each with their own techniques and motifs. Whether antique or newly made, this pottery is highly collectible. We purchased the jardiniere shown on the previous page at a collegiate rummage sale for $10. It is versatile for potted plants or fresh floral designs.

Business and Corporate Gifts

Plants and flowers make great gifts for anyone, especially those who seem to have everything. Men and women alike enjoy the beauty of a live, healthy plant, so consider this a great gift idea. A poinsettia in bloom is bright and festive and adds energy to the office.

Research has shown plants increase productivity in the workplace. Why not prepare a plant in holiday trims for your work colleague and deliver it to them personally? Another option is to contact your local florist and have a holiday poinsettia sent to the workplace "just because."

Corporate gifts are important expressions during the holiday season. Reward special clients with a commanding basket of rose and burgundy poinsettias that they can enjoy for the entire season. Flowers show you care and express sentiments that are challenging to put into words. When making your gift list, consider flowers and plants!

Pocketbook of Posies

A woman on the go, who loves to travel, may slow down her pace to embrace this mossy satchel filled with Princettia Pink® blooms. The plants, cut Momi fir, and container were grown and/or made in Mississippi. This design would make an attractive gift as well as a smart display item in a boutique or hotel.

Dried Floral Pot

Dried flowers provide long-lasting displays of form and texture in designs. Flower farmers often grow versatile flower crops that are attractive in both their fresh form and dried.

In this example, we used dried flowers in a playful combination with smooth, matte-leaved poinsettia plants. We grew a color mix of *Xerochrysum bracteatum* (straw flower) during the summer, harvesting just the flower heads in their already dry, papery state. We attached the flower heads to a glass cube vase using hot glue, then set 4-inch-diameter plants inside. The results are charming and quite unexpected.

White Linen

Don't forget to add decoration to the bath. Small poinsettias take up so little room yet provide more than their size in holiday cheer.

Into the Woodland

Poinsettias can be considered formal flowers. Their floral parts are well-organized, and new varieties like this Princettia Pure White® have uniform growth and form. It is fun to contrast these plants with informal elements such as this bark-and-moss planter.

In this design, we see something different in terms of the element of *proportion*. Many floral enthusiasts learn early in their practice to make a flower arrangement one and a half to two times the height of the container, but here, we've done the opposite. A practical outcome of this technique is that the design makes a terrific table centerpiece because guests can easily see one another over the flower arrangement. The design provides a feeling of comfort because the plants are nestled snugly in their bed of forest moss.

THANK YOU

Beaumont Horticultural Unit

Chelsealea Lovell

David Mills, The Nature of Things, Courtland, Mississippi

Dixie Butler

Doyle's Coastal Ridge Flower Farm, Picayune, Mississippi

MSU Coastal Research and Extension Center Staff

MSU Extension Master Floral Designers

MSU Extension Master Gardeners

Ralph Null, Professor Emeritus, Mississippi State University

South Mississippi Branch Experiment Station Staff

Tanis Clifton, Happy Trails Flower Farm, Dennis, Mississippi